DIVINE
PROVISION
MEETS GENEROSITY
PLANNING

HOW TO LIVE LIFE TO THE FULLEST
WHILE RICHLY GIVING

Divine Provision Meets Generosity Planning

How to Live Life to the Fullest While Richly Giving

INTERSECTION

Where God's Wealth Meets God's Wisdom

JOHNNY MCWILLIAMS

Zero In Financial Press

Myrtle Beach, South Carolina

Zero In Financial Press
PO BOX 1718
Myrtle Beach, SC 29578
United States of America

Full Disclosure: Some of the links in this book and related materials may be affiliate links (excluding any and all links to Amazon), and we may earn a small commission when you make a purchase through them, at no additional cost to you. By FTC law we must disclose this. However, we want to assure you that we only endorse products and services we believe in and would or do use ourselves.

Divine Provision Meets Generosity Planning, How to Live Life to the Fullest While Richly Giving / Series: INTERSECTION, Where God's Wealth Meets God's Wisdom / Johnny McWilliams, author.

Hardback ISBN-13: 978-1-954485-15-0
Paperback ISBN-13: 978-1-954485-16-7
E-book (EPUB) ISBN-13: 978-1-954485-17-4
E-book (PDF) ISBN-13: 978-1-954485-19-8
Library of Congress Control Number: 2022908987

Access free resources mentioned in this book:
intersection.zeroinfinancial.com

Editor: Fleur Marie Vaz, fleurmarievaz@gmail.com
Additional Editing: Melanie Brown
Cover image design: Edgar Rios, edgrrr5@gmail.com

Note: Scripture quotations in which certain words are bold are the author's emphasis added.

Contents

Dedication

I dedicate this book series to my Lord and Savior, Jesus Christ, who has carried me, walked with me, and led me all the way to completion. Thank You for always being the God who always keeps His promises.

> *And the Lord, he it is that doth go before thee; he will be with thee, he will not fail thee, neither forsake thee: fear not, neither be dismayed (Deuteronomy 31:8).*

Acknowledgments

I want to acknowledge and thank my best friend and incredible wife, Christine. Your undying support never ceases to amaze me. You have stood by me through it all. I couldn't have finished this project without you.

Thank you to my children, Seth and Paige. I love you and am so proud to be your dad. Your faith in Christ and success in life have been a beautiful display of God's grace.

Thank you to my parents, Clovers and Val McWilliams. You have always been a rock of consistent encouragement, believing in me throughout the decades. You both have faithfully studied the Word of God and have inspired me to do the same. Your prayers have kept blessings pouring out upon my life.

Thank you to my Pastor for over a decade, Al Toledo, for your powerful teaching and ministry that will always have a lasting influence on my business and writing. And to my current Pastor, Chris Honeycutt, who has been abundantly supportive as I worked through the last twelve months of this project.

Free Resources

To help you Zero In on the INTERSECTION where God's Wealth meets God's Wisdom, download the free resources from the INTERSECTION Resource Page:

intersection.zeroinfinancial.com

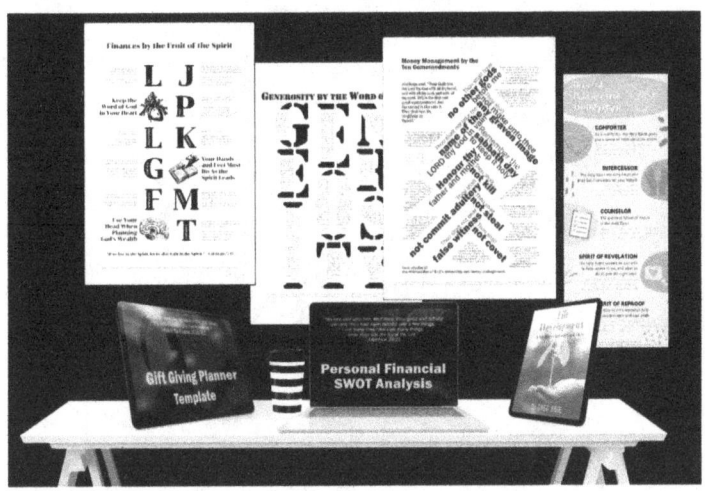

- **BOOK:** Life Development—A New Believer's Guide to Growing in Christ

- **INFOGRAPHIC:** Financial Guidance from the Holy Spirit

- **POSTER:** Finances by the Fruit of the Spirit

- **WORKBOOK:** Personal Financial SWOT Analysis

- **POSTER:** Money Management by the Ten Commandments

- **WORKBOOK:** Gift Giving Planner Template

- **POSTER:** Generosity by the Word of God

Zero In On Giving

I admit it. Giving is my favorite way to use money. I am a giver by nature. This is not the case for all people, and that is totally okay. Some people are natural savers and investors, for example, and that is an amazing natural talent to have. But just like I had to learn and intentionally focus on saving, everyone needs to have generosity in their lives, even if it is not their first instinct.

Also, I am a natural spender. Exchanging money for stuff and experiences energizes me. Only instead of buying things for myself, I also like to buy for others. Most givers are spenders as well, so this may be something you can relate to.

However, the natural savers in my life taught me an important principle: the more you save today, the more you will have to give tomorrow. And in return, I could impart my way of thinking, helping them realize the joy of generosity. That really helped me see that we both have strengths, just different strengths. Neither way is better. Everyone needs to understand how to take advantage of their strengths to get better at their weaknesses.

After I realized God owns everything, which I present in *God's Ownership Meets Money Management*, it hit me: God gave to me, so that I can give to others. Giving is exciting, but giving someone else's stuff is even more exhilarating for me. And, since God owns it all, and I really own nothing, that is the case every time I give! So, it may come as no surprise that this is my favorite INTERSECTION of all.

Divine Provision Meets Generosity Planning is all about why we give, where we give, and how we give God's Wealth. This is by far the most fun you can have with money; but it goes far beyond monetary giving.

Since we all have strengths and weaknesses, plus we tend towards particular money management behaviors, we must explore the DNA of giving first. Chapters 1 through 3 will walk through giving since the beginning of time and why we are wired to enjoy this amazing act. This will lay a firm foundation on which we can build a plan to systematically give. Part I will show you *why*.

The middle of this book will be very strategic. If you ever wanted to know how to give a ton without spending much money, there will be several strategies presented for you. Also, don't miss the accompanying resources which will help you plan through all the gift-giving events in your life. Part II will show you *how*.

The third part of the book will dive into *where* giving fits in the budget. It takes you through the basics of budgeting generosity, then goes into specific budgeting tactics for the three ways to give. Last, you will find some places where you can find the greatest examples of giving in the Word of God.

This book of the series is to get you hungry to learn more and explore beyond these principles. It is only a primer for building a lifelong love for liberality.

So, are you ready for an exciting journey? I hope so, because God created you for this ultimate duty.

Part I

Giving is in Our DNA

CHAPTER ONE

God is a Giver

God made us in His image, and He is the biggest giver of all. So, it makes sense to look towards God's example first, so we can study His pattern of generosity. Then we can use His wealth, the provisions He has allowed us to manage, the way He has taught us by His Wisdom.

It is also important to note that God gives with no strings attached. He embeds within us a purpose, and through that career or ministry, and with those skills and talents, we receive His abundant provision. Yes, we have fun doing what we were made to do, and then He gives us more than we deserve.

His provision is free indeed, and we must give with the same love and mindset. It goes back to the Holy Spirit leading your financial heart, hands+feet, and head, which you read about in: *Biblical Faith Meets Financial Strategy.*

Finally, it is important to realize that you don't deserve God's gifts. You will see that God gives to us when we praise Him as well as when we have done nothing but turn our backs on Him. This is mysterious and feels awkward to our way of thinking.

We live in a "this-for-that" world. In every area of life, you see people give only if they know they will get something in return. There are those who give out of guilt and pressure to give. And we see an attitude of entitlement at every turn. Let's check our motives and understand another way our Maker wants us to distribute His wealth.

The generosity examples God displays and presents in His Word are for us to understand giving in its purest form. We must continually pray for His guidance in giving, but don't hesitate to turn to His blueprint in the Bible. So, let's look at God as the Greatest Giver of all time.

Generosity from the Beginning

God has been giving from the beginning of creation. He made Eden just for humankind, and it is very apparent that Eden was a spectacular garden, an experience we will have to wait until heaven to experience again. If I let my imagination run wild, I imagine the most beautiful array of flowers, plants, and trees we have never seen since the beginning. We know there was no disease, weeds, or mold. It even had an automatic sprinkler system naturally built into the ground. God hooked Adam and Eve up with the best of the best.

One tree God gave them was right in the middle of the garden and was very special. It was the Tree of Life, a tree that had leaves of healing and immortality.

At the same time, our Creator gave us work. As you read in *God's Ownership Meets Money Management*, God owns everything, so just as our very life is a gift, so is our job. We see how being idle causes physical, mental, and spiritual fatigue. So, without this gift, our lives would start to deteriorate. Thank God for this gift of being productive!

Then, if we dedicate our lives and our work unto the Lord, He gives us a reward for that, called profit. It's unbelievable that the more we use God's gifts, the more blessings we receive. Proverbs 14:23 says, "In all labour there is profit."

Even after Adam and Eve sinned, hid from their Father and Creator, and played the blame game, God was so generous by making them clothing. These garments were the first clothes in history yet another gift from God. Think about it; He could have left them embarrassed, naked, and ashamed, gathering itchy leaves to cover themselves; but not our Loving Father. The Greatest Giver could never let that happen. Instead, He provided the world's first leather apparel from the skins of animals.

After these initial days in history, God continues to give. One of the greatest gifts ever is His promise. A research paper states: "Everett R. Storms, a schoolteacher in Canada, who made a detailed study of promises ... came up with a grand total of ... 7,487 ... promises made by God to humankind."[1] And He always keeps His promises. The only obligation on our part is to accept the gift.

He promised Noah protection from His wrath upon the world. The Lord appeared to Abraham and promised to make him a great nation. God promised Moses guidance and wisdom as he led all the Israelites to the Promised Land. He even gave them all water, bread, and meat from heaven during the many years of wilderness. Those are gifts of protection, prosperity, and provision!

As God led Moses, and the nation of Israel, out of Egypt, He used this moment of deliverance to teach them how to give each other exceptional gifts.

"And if thy brother be waxen poor, and fallen in decay with thee; then thou shalt relieve him: yea, though he be a stranger, or a sojourner; that he may live with thee. Take thou no usury of him, or increase: but fear thy God; that thy brother may live with thee. Thou shalt not give him thy money upon usury, nor lend him thy victuals for increase. I am the Lord your God, which brought you forth out of the land of Egypt, to give you the land of Canaan, and to be your God" (Leviticus 25:35-38).

So, God used His gift of Canaan, the Promised Land, to teach them how to take care of those who had fallen on hard times. He instructs them to be merciful to each other, giving whatever is needed, including food to eat, a place to sleep, or money for their necessities. Giving to homeless and downtrodden people should be something we feel led to do throughout our lives.

There is a warning in this passage that I believe is important not to miss. God mentions twice: do not give expecting that this is an investment for personal gain. Because the Israelites were recipients of His generosity, they were to reciprocate that display of love. Gifts are to be free of charge.

Be careful to check yourself when giving. Don't let pride get a hold of you so that you expect to receive something back from those to whom you have shared. Even staying away from the temptation to seek praise or adoration is important when being genuinely generous.

Neither should you expect a standing ovation and a plaque with your name. All you need to know is that your Father in heaven sees what you do and that He is pleased with your donations, offerings, and gifts. As Jesus said: "But when thou doest alms, let not thy left hand know what thy right hand doeth: That thine alms may be in secret: and thy Father which seeth in secret himself shall reward thee openly" (Matthew 6:3-4). And, Jesus knows all about giving.

He Gave His All

You can ask almost any random person whether they have heard this verse, and they will most likely say yes. Even if they have never picked up a Bible in their life, they have seen or heard someone quote it. If you Google "Most Quoted Bible Verses," you will get many lists in the search results, and this verse is always near the top. It may be the most quoted verse of all time.

"For God so loved the world, that **He gave His only begotten Son**, that whosoever believeth in Him should not perish, but **have everlasting life**" (John 3:16).

Even if you are a natural giver as I am, could you imagine giving your one and only son? God did that for you and me, so we could have everlasting life. That's a double gift! Our loving Father is perfect and cannot allow us in our sinful state to live with Him in heaven. There had to be a blood sacrifice for forgiveness, but the blood of an animal had no staying power. To ensure total remission of our sins, the sinless Lamb was the only way.

If it were up to me in my fallen human nature, I would have thought about letting sinful humans get what they rightfully deserve: hell. I would have thought about flushing this whole thing down the toilet and starting over again, maybe taking away the freewill given to mankind and forcing us to love, obey, and give thanks. But not our Heavenly Father.

God loves us so much He gave us this most unbelievable gift. And salvation is *100%* free: He wants nothing in return. If you think you are a great giver, top that! It's been said many times: you can't out give God.

Once again, God made us in His image; He wants us to use His example as our giving model, surrendering our vengeance mindset for love.

You may have John 3:16 memorized, but do you have 1 John 3:16 committed to memory? The New Living Translation says, "We know what real love is because Jesus gave up his life for us. So we also ought to give up our lives for our brothers and sisters" (1 John 3:16).

As you continue to study this passage, you find John writes how we are identified as children of God by our giving to those in need. We cannot have fellowship with Jesus if we are not following His example. You might not have to die for your brother or sister physically, but you must show compassion when they are in need.

As I presented in the resource *Money Management by the Ten Commandments*, the law says not to covet. And here we see an even greater commandment: love says that not coveting is not enough; to love is to give as He gave.

One teaching of Jesus was the story of the Good Samaritan. You may have heard this story before but not thought about it in the context of giving. Jesus was teaching a lesson on giving to a man who was an expert on the religious law. So, this example He gave was tailor-made for him with his knowledge and preconceived notions.

We know what real love is because Jesus gave up his life for us. So we also ought to give up our lives for our brothers and sisters

(1 John 3:16 NLT).

A traveling man was robbed, stripped of his clothing, and badly injured. Laying on the side of the road, he was in desperate need. Two persons walked by not offering to help. The story even says that they crossed over to the other side of the road so they wouldn't have to entertain the sight of this helpless man (Luke 10:25-37).

How many times have you seen someone in a dire situation, but you had somewhere to be, so you avoided even passing near? Have you ever received a call from a friend or family member asking for help, but you put them off, avoiding later phone calls?

Then, the story continues; a Samaritan sees the man and helps him. He doesn't just do the minimum; he goes above and beyond. The man receives the medical care, food, and clothing he needs. The Good Samaritan also provides transportation to a lodging place, so the man could recuperate from his injuries. Then this generous person pays the hotel bill for as long as the man needed to stay.

The Samaritan must have had the means to do all of this, meaning I would assume this man was wealthy. This story shows the purpose of wealth: serving others, sharing with those in need, providing for people who cannot help themselves.

Also, notice how this story disrupts the incorrect thinking that being rich is evil. If only evil people were rich, who would have the resource to be outrageously generous? Giving as our Savior has given is the most fulfilling thing we can do with money, time, talent, energy, and other resources we have been provided.

Jesus is the King of kings. Remember, He was in heaven on the throne before the world began. Jesus left real wealth, which we cannot even comprehend, to come to earth, putting on humanity, living with common people, and to give his life for us. He has shown what giving everything looks like from a position of the highest wealth.

He gave His all. And then He concludes by saying, "Go, and do thou likewise."

He Keeps on Giving

"Since he did not spare even his own Son but gave him up for us all, won't he also give us everything else?" (Romans 8:32 NLT)

God has a past full of examples of giving. And He has promises of giving that reach far into the future. One of the last commandments Jesus gave His disciples while walking the earth was to wait on yet another great gift. Yes, after He just gave His life, the greatest gift anyone could ever receive, He promises an encore. Crazy!

Remember the Holy Spirit, the third person of the Godhead? Yes, Jesus promises you will receive the Holy Spirit, who will live in you and live through you all the days of your life once you have accepted salvation. This promise is a multi-faceted gift that comes with great power.

Look at the Holy Spirit's line-up of supernatural gifts for you: the *Revelatory* gifts of Word of wisdom, word of knowledge, discerning of spirits; the *Healing* gifts of faith, healing, miracles; and the *Vocal* gifts of tongues, interpretation of tongues, and prophecy.

> *For to one is given by the Spirit the word of wisdom; to another the word of knowledge by the same Spirit; To another faith by the same Spirit; to another the gifts of healing by the same Spirit; To another the working of miracles; to another prophecy; to another discerning of spirits; to another divers kinds of tongues; to another the interpretation of tongues (1 Corinthians 12:8-10).*

The Holy Spirit equips us, so that we can continue the work of preaching the word with signs, wonders and miracles following, just as Jesus did.

Have you ever received a gift, opened the package, looked at it, and thought, "How in the world do I use this?" That's how most people feel when they look at this list. But, thank God, they come with the instruction manual. The Holy Spirit will help you as you grow deeper in using these gifts. Phew! I know; I feel relieved too.

I have a resource for you which you can use to realize financial guidance by the Holy Spirit. You may remember this from *Biblical Faith Meets Financial Strategy*. So, once you have bowed your heart to God and dedicated your life to

Jesus Christ, you have a wonderful gift waiting for you, and this infographic only shows you a portion of this glorious reward.

You can download it from the INTERSECTION resource page: intersection.zeroinfinancial.com.

But wait, there's more! He keeps the best gifts for last. There is a reward for our patience and endurance until the end. Here in Revelation, the last book of the Bible, there is a list of gifts for those who overcome and are faithful to the end. Finishing this race is a big deal.

"…To him that overcometh will **I give to eat of the tree of life**, which is in the midst of the paradise of God" (Revelation 2:7).

"…be thou faithful unto death, and **I will give thee a crown of life**" (Revelation 2:10).

"…To him that overcometh will **I give to eat of the hidden manna**, and will **give him a white stone**, and in the stone a new name written, which no man knoweth saving he that receiveth it" (Revelation 2:17).

Life is not always going to be a cakewalk, but God has given us all we need, if we only trust in Him. Then He goes beyond and gives us divine provisions to live and give exceedingly. And when we complete the race and cross the finish line, we can enjoy the gift we have been waiting for since the beginning of time.

Yes, there it is: the Tree of Life God gave Adam and Eve in the beginning. It has been preserved for us all this time. And there is the manna God served Moses and the

Israelites while wandering in the desert. You will also receive a crown of life, a unique personalized engraved stone, and many other incredible gifts.

These are mysterious gifts we will not fully understand until that day. This celebration is going to be like nothing we can even comprehend. But the ironic thing is, I don't think any of these gifts will mesmerize us more than beholding the One who gave it all. Jesus is, for sure, going to steal the show. He was, is, and will always be the Greatest Gift of all.

I love the way Randy Alcorn describes that day: "The most astonishing sight we can anticipate in Heaven is not streets of gold or pearly gates or loved ones who've died before us. It will be coming face-to-face with our Savior. To look into Jesus' eyes will be to see what we've always longed to see: the person who made us and for whom we were made. And we'll see Him in the place He made for us and for which we were made. Seeing God will be like seeing everything else for the first time."[2]

Jesus was not only the greatest gift over two thousand years ago, but He is also the greatest gift today, and He will be the greatest gift in the afterlife. You must understand that without this Gift, no other gift really matters. And I can't write another word without making sure you have received the free gift of salvation.

Don't worry if you feel you don't deserve it—no one does. And don't believe the lie that you are not ready and one day you will be in the right situation. Today is the day.

I would like to lead you in prayer. There is nothing mysterious about these words, and you must mean them wholeheartedly; so, please, make them your own. I only want to provide you with a template, a place to start, if you don't know what to say. These words are from the sinner's prayer that Billy Graham would use to lead someone as they pray for salvation.[3]

So, bow your head and your heart, and if you believe these words, Jesus will forever change your life.

> *Dear Lord Jesus, I know that I am a sinner, and I ask for Your forgiveness. I believe You died for my sins and rose from the dead. I turn from my sins and invite You to come into my heart and life. I want to trust and follow You as my Lord and Savior. In Your Name. Amen*

If you have made this decision today, I would like to know, plus I would like to send you a gift to help you in your walk with Christ. Go to salvation.zeroinfinancial.com to declare your decision to follow Jesus, and grab this resource that is especially tailored to help you live at the INTERSECTION of God's amazing salvation and your humble decision.

The gift I would like to send you is an indispensable resource. My dear friend, accountability partner, and fellow

author, Pastor D. Greg Ebie has allowed me to distribute his book, "Life Development—A New Believer's Guide to Growing in Christ," to anyone who declares their life in Christ. I would like to thank him not only for writing this amazing book, but also for allowing me to provide it to you.

I really wanted to share something that would help you grow your faith in Jesus Christ because Biblical Faith is the only way to develop a reliable Financial Strategy. Get ready to be challenged as you work your way through Pastor Greg's foundational guide.

Grab your copy of this study guide and have your Bible in hand! Download it today: salvation.zeroinfinancial.com[4]

CHAPTER TWO

The Gift Received When Giving

Never give with an attitude of quid pro quo but know that there is a reward received when giving that is wonderfully unexpected. Also, I am not referring to *The Gift of Giving*, which is one of the special attributes of the Holy Spirit. Rather this chapter is about the bonus received when being generous.

The golden rule works because there is a built-in reciprocity that occurs when you do unto others as you would have them do unto you. And once you see how fun and rewarding giving is, it becomes addictive.

WARNING: It's a shame that I must put this cautionary note here, but I must say it one more time. Some give with the wrong motive. As I mention, some share their heavenly resources with the expectation of receiving something in return. Don't fall into this trap because it will backfire.

In his book *Give and Take*, Adam Grant recommends that companies consciously develop giving as a reciprocity style for the whole organization by recognizing and rewarding givers. An article on Success.com, which mentions Grant's book, states, "We want something for our giving, if only recognition; better yet, a decent quid pro quo. No matter how rewarding pure generosity can be, somewhere below the surface—and often not very far—sits a gremlin with an accounting ledger, encouraging you to ask, 'What's in it for me?'"[1]

As you can see, the world's view is that you should expect something in return for giving because that is our base human nature. The author even refers to our desires as coming from a gremlin, some mischievous imp we cannot control. The article concludes by quoting Grant, "You can't change human nature ..." They are absolutely correct: you can't. But God can.

"Every generous act and every perfect gift is from above, coming down from the Father of lights" (James 1:17a HCSB).

The only way to truly be generous with your possessions is to give with no expectation of recompense.

That includes a gift in return, a "thank you," and any praise whatsoever. God should get all the glory. It is all His anyway.

Tim Keller, pastor, theologian, and Christian apologist once said, "A lack of generosity refuses to acknowledge that your assets are not really yours, but God's."

With that said, there are benefits that are too good to be ignored, and you should enjoy the fruit of giving.

> *"In all of my years of service to my Lord, I have discovered a truth that has never failed and has never been compromised. That truth is that it is beyond the realm of possibilities that one has the ability to out give God. Even if I give the whole of my worth to Him, He will find a way to give back to me much more than I gave" (Charles Spurgeon).*

The Gift You Get Today

There is a fantastic feeling you get when you give. It is like an emotional hug or spiritual kiss; some describe it as warm fuzzies. I had to look up the definition of "warm fuzzies," and the dictionary confirmed that this phrase sums up this unique sensation.

warm fuzzies: plural noun—feelings of happiness, contentment, or sentimentality[2]

The bottom line is, you will experience a "high" better than any drug could ever give you.

Givers may even get more out of the transaction than the receiver. Jesus taught, it is better to give than receive (Acts 20:35) for a reason. There is a joy in sharing that is felt immediately. If you don't believe me, try it.

Have you ever left a twenty-dollar bill to pay for the next person in line at the coffee shop? And then you whisper to the barista, "Don't tell the person why their coffee is free, and the rest of the money is yours to keep." You get a big smile from the barista, which makes you feel good, and now you get to sit back and watch how it unfolds while waiting for your beverage!

Your coffee will never taste better than it does on that day. Just find a spot on a stool and enjoy, but don't make it too obvious. The next person in line will do what everyone does. They look around, trying to spot the secret day-maker. As you nonchalantly read your magazine, tap away on your laptop, scroll on your mobile phone, or inconspicuously stare at the wall, know you have made someone's day.

Even better; try paying for someone's groceries. You can tell how financially strapped the person is by the size of the smile or even the embrace you get in return. That's one of the best gifts of giving. This will not be so covert and is such a big deal, but you must make sure to not do it with the wrong motive.

I've heard stories of this tremendous act of generosity ending up with some pretty spectacular reactions. That single mom may be in tears. The cashier may not stop freaking out. The whole checkout line may erupt in applause. I've even heard of it becoming spontaneously contagious where the next line over does the same, and the one beyond them repeats the gesture. That's giving gone wild!

Get creative and test out this phenomenon! Fill up someone's gas tank and wash their windows. Carry someone's heavy package up to their apartment, leaving it outside their door, so they don't have to go down to pick it up in the lobby.

An article in Psychological Science states: "In two studies, psychology researchers Ed O'Brien (University of Chicago Booth School of Business) and Samantha Kassirer (Northwestern University Kellogg School of Management) found that participants' happiness did not decline, or declined much slower, if they repeatedly bestowed gifts on others versus repeatedly receiving those same gifts themselves."[3]

You will never regret giving. The more often you give, the better it gets. The opposite happens for the recipient. When someone receives, there is a need for a bit more every time in the future for the happiness to stay consistent. God wired us that way.

There is a sense of pleasure you will get when shopping for, or creating, or performing the gift. The thought process you must go through to prepare makes you get excited about blessing the recipient. You've heard that it's the thought that counts; well, it turns out that the thinking process matters too. The thought counts more for the giver than the receiver.

Then there are the moments leading up to giving. Is it a surprise gift? Or is the gift expected, but you plan for it to exceed their expectations?

Endorphins are released as the moment approaches, giving you a rush that can't be put into words. Your palms get sweaty, and you don't know why. It's not like you are doing anything daring like jumping from an airplane. This is not a once in a lifetime event like popping the question. But the rush is almost just the same.

It is not only the smile, the hug, or the "thank you" you get back. Even anonymous gifts bring a heightened sense of pleasure that receiving a gift cannot match.

It is not even the amount of money it costs you. We will look at ways you can give that cost little money (if any at all) in Part II. And these gifts yield as much—and even more—appreciation as the expensive ones.

Anyway, it is a blast, and I don't know if I can do it much justice in these pages. It would help if you experienced this benefit for yourself.

And if you want to get the most out of it, wait until you are having a not-so-great day. Then, instead of being moody and blue, go give something small to someone who is not expecting it. You may even choose someone else who is not having a great day. Watch what happens; you will be pleasantly surprised by how the rest of your day goes, especially when you do it for them and not for what you hope to receive. Both of your spirits will be lifted. It's a win-win.

The Gift You Get Tomorrow

People remember a giver. Again, you don't want to give to be admired for your giving, but your gifts will be top of mind when *you* are in need. There is an expression that says: "What goes around comes around." That expression works for good and for bad.

I remember having someone complaining to me about being stranded on the side of the road, and no one came to his rescue. He called people for help, but no one responded. Hazard lights continued to blink, but no cars were stopping to assist.

After I inquired why he thought this was the case. He exclaimed, "Because people are selfish." So, I politely asked him, "How often have you helped others who are in need?" Maybe there was someone who needed a ride. Or maybe there was someone homeless begging for something to eat. He stood silently.

I don't believe in karma. That is a wicked spiritual principle of cause and effect rooted in lies of incarnation and a mindset that guarantees justice by some unknown force. The Bible says God provides rain and sunshine for the just and the unjust the same. But I see the evidence of the gift of giving that comes tomorrow, meaning at some future point in time.

A lady I know wanted to give something to a fellow church member who was in her last month of pregnancy. The soon-to-be mother seemed so tired and had issues getting around and doing basic things. So, the lady went over and spent her afternoon serving her sister, giving her an at-home pedicure. The pregnant woman was so grateful. (That's the gift today.)

Years later, the new mom still talks about this gift she received and tells the story to her friends and family. That sweet, generous lady now has the respect and admiration of many people. It turns out that it was a gift that keeps on giving back! (That's the gift tomorrow.)

Sometimes the gift that the giver gets is unexpected and far greater than the original present. As you can see, this works not only for presents that cost money but also for time and talent gifts.

The Bible has much to say about the blessing you will receive when giving to the neediest people in your community and the world. By the way, this is one of the many promises that God gives us:

> *Blessed is he that considereth the poor: the Lord will deliver him in time of trouble. The Lord will preserve him, and keep him alive; and he shall be blessed upon the earth: and thou wilt not*

deliver him unto the will of his enemies. The
Lord will strengthen him upon the bed of
languishing: thou wilt make all his bed in his
sickness (Psalm 41:1-3).

What a promise! The truth of the scripture debunks all "this-for-that" thinking, where the reward equals the generosity. We see here that when you give to the poor, you get deliverance from trouble, protection from enemies, healing from sickness, and the blessing of the Lord. God gives you far more than you gave because He is God, and His ways are not our ways. Those are some outrageous gifts.

Notice once again, your generosity can go far beyond things that cost you money. The following passage lumps your financial gifts in with giving others forgiveness.

"Be ye therefore merciful, as your Father also is merciful. Judge not, and ye shall not be judged: condemn not, and ye shall not be condemned: forgive, and ye shall be forgiven: **Give, and it shall be given unto you; good measure, pressed down, and shaken together, and running over**, shall men give into your bosom. For with the same measure that ye mete withal it shall be measured to you again" (Luke 6:36-38).

That phrase "good measure, pressed down, and shaken together, and running over" means you are getting back far more than you gave. Think of filling a jar with flour and then, when it is full, pressing it down to make

Money is not bad,

for it is necessary

to do many good things

in this world.

room for more. Then shake the container until it all settles down, and all the air is out of it; then fill it up to the brim. Do it again and keep doing it until you can't fit anymore in the jar. Now keep pouring until it spills all over onto the floor. That's the picture of the gift you will get in return.

But please don't do it for the overflow. Give out of the goodness of your heart. Then you get a gift beyond tomorrow.

The Gift You Get Beyond Tomorrow

There is one more layer to the reward that comes back to the giver. And it is the grandest.

In the following passage of scripture, Jesus is explaining that there will be a tremendous gift waiting for those in heaven who stored up treasures there. This reality is mysterious to us because we can't envision or imagine heaven in all of its glory. But by keeping this truth in mind, it can change our habits and enhance our giving mindset.

"Lay not up for yourselves treasures upon earth, where moth and rust doth corrupt, and where thieves break through and steal: But **lay up for yourselves treasures in heaven**, where neither moth nor rust doth corrupt, and where thieves do not break through nor steal: **For where your treasure is, there will your heart be also**" (Matthew 6:19-21).

This teaching should not be taken lightly. Your actions with money affect your heart is many ways, and its health subsequently guides your entire financial life. Positioning your heart is vitally important. (Read *Biblical Faith Meets Financial Strategy* where I walk the reader through how to take care of the financial heart.)

Commentary from The Bible Says states:

> *Continuing His instruction on how to seek their best, Jesus warns His disciples not to store up for yourselves treasures on earth. Treasure can be anything someone highly values. Treasures are precious. They can be money, time, relationships, reputations, accomplishments, etc. The reason He warns against this is that all treasures on earth will one day lose their value. It is an inferior investment strategy to store up (save or invest) anything of considerable value in a place where it is likely to be ruined or lost.*
>
> *And here is the kicker. It is not only a wise investment to store lasting treasures through obedience to God, and seeking to please Him. It also properly orients your heart. Jesus reveals a core reason His disciples should store up treasures in heaven is because of this truth: where your treasure is, there your heart will be as well.*
>
> *Our hearts always follow what we treasure. If we store our treasures on earth, we not only lose our treasure, we also fill our heart with the things of a world that will one day be no more.*[4]

So, let's look at three things that you can do while on earth to store up treasure in heaven. The first one—you guessed it—is giving. But Jesus explains that there is a particular way to give. This mindset goes back to what I said about sharing in the right way. It would be best if you gave expecting nothing in return.

If you don't get a "Thank You," you should keep giving, anyway. No smile? No hug? No praise? Keep on giving. No gift today or tomorrow? Don't worry; you have treasures waiting for you beyond tomorrow.

When you receive the joy of those gifts today and tomorrow in return for your generosity, those are just a bonus. The proper reward will be waiting for you after you leave this life.

Because we give with no expectation of anything in return, this is just something we know in the back of our minds and should not affect what, how much, or when we give. I love this story Pastor Cole used in a sermon:

> There's a story about a stingy Scotsman who accidentally tossed a crown into the collection plate, thinking it was a penny. When he saw his mistake, he asked to have it back. The deacon refused, so the Scotsman consoled himself by saying, "Aweel, aweel, I'll get credit for it in heaven." The deacon responded, "Na, na, ye'll get credit for the penny." [5]

The second way is to lead someone to Christ. It will take time away from something you want to do for yourself, I'm sure. And when you reach out to the lost, all kinds of distractions will pop up to prevent you from this great commission. You will have resistance.

You will store up treasure in heaven when you dedicate time to witness to others about your transformed life. Also, you receive some of those gifts today that I mentioned above. Your heart will race with joy when someone bows their head, and you have the privilege of leading them in the sinner's prayer. There is no greater joy. I'll go much deeper into this way of building heavenly rewards in Chapter 7.

The third way to lay up wealth for the afterlife is to give your entire life over to the ministry of Jesus Christ. There is no more excellent way to give. I am not in full-time ministry per se, but I fully dedicate my business to God. I pray He uses every opportunity through this company to proclaim His goodness, His generosity, and His precious gift of salvation.

Those that have given their entire life to the ministry have the ultimate calling. Please provide for missionaries and pastors you know and love; many of them need more support for the ever-growing needs they are fulfilling.

Ministers of the Gospel have a gift waiting in heaven for their incredible sacrifice. They are the under-shepherd, and Jesus, the Great Shepherd, will be waiting for them when they have finished their service.

The Bible says, "Feed the flock of God which is among you, taking the oversight thereof, not by constraint, but willingly; not for filthy lucre, but of a ready mind … And when the chief Shepherd shall appear, **ye shall receive a crown of glory that fadeth not away**" (1 Peter 5:2,4).

The phrase "not for filthy lucre" is commanding that they do not do it just for the money. Compensation is described as filthy because, compared to the gift in heaven, it is rubbish. Remember that money is not bad, for it is necessary to do many good things in this world.

So, when you give, no matter if it's money, time, talent, or your own life, do it unto God, and you will receive more than you can imagine today, tomorrow, and beyond tomorrow.

CHAPTER THREE

Why Offerings?

Throughout the Bible, you will read about offerings. Remember that tithes are not offerings, and that distinction is made many times in the Bible. The tithe is not a gift. Go read about returning the tithe in *God's Ownership Meets Money Management*. Tithing is a manager's responsibility, while your offerings come from generosity.

Offerings are gifts to God's church above and beyond the tithe. You return the tithe, and you give an offering. There are many occasions on which you may bring an offering to the church. But God wants to make sure you understand something first.

Asaph wrote a Psalm where he describes a funny scene in which Israel was getting a bit cocky. Imagine you are bringing an offering to the church, and you were feeling pretty generous today. Just in case you thought that you were giving God something out of your abundance, God says:

> *I will take no bullock out of thy house, nor he goats out of thy folds. For every beast of the forest is mine, and the cattle upon a thousand hills. I know all the fowls of the mountains: and the wild beasts of the field are mine. If I were hungry, I would not tell thee: for the world is mine, and the fulness thereof (Psalm 50:9-12).*

It has been said many times, and I'll say it right here and now: neither God nor His church needs any money from us! "He is the God who made the world and everything in it. Since he is Lord of heaven and earth, he doesn't live in man-made temples, and human hands can't serve his needs—for he has no needs. He himself gives life and breath to everything, and he satisfies every need" (Acts 17:24-25 NLT).

Then why should we ever give an offering to the God who has no hardships? Giving an offering is more for your blessing than for God's benefit. And, He allows you to decide how to manage and what to do with all you have after tithes and taxes. Your generosity is on full display with this wealth. Charities, birthday gifts, and offerings all happen here.

"Every man **according as he purposeth in his heart,** so let him give; not grudgingly, or of necessity: for God loveth a cheerful giver" (2 Corinthians 9:7).

As I've heard in church many times, this should not be a moment of pressure. You have heard it quoted many times that God loves a cheerful giver, but don't miss the words just before this phrase: "not grudgingly, or of necessity." If you are giving with the mindset of, "I have to … or else …" it may not be worth doing. The definition of "grudgingly" is "in a way that is given or done unwillingly."[1] If you are giving unwillingly, reluctantly, or sparingly, don't give. God says so.

But when you give with a thankful and cheerful heart, of course, God promises to give back. Give generously, and God blesses you with even more.

"There is that scattereth, and yet increaseth; and there is that withholdeth more than is meet, but it tendeth to poverty. **The liberal soul shall be made fat: and he that watereth shall be watered also himself**" (Proverbs 11:24-25).

Don't worry; this is the healthy kind of fat, also translated as "prosperous." The word "prosperity" gets a bad rap due to those who are greedy or prideful. I feel like I keep repeating myself—maybe that's because I am. But, I must reiterate that you do not give to become profitable, but God blesses those who provide gifts with the correct intentions.

I'm always in awe of the story of Solomon, who was quite possibly the wealthiest person to ever live. It is written: "In Gibeon the Lord appeared to Solomon in a dream by night: and God said, Ask what I shall give thee" (1 Kings 3:5).

I've always contemplated what I would say at this point. Well, Solomon answered by requesting wisdom, which we know he received abundantly. God will forever grant your request when it aligns with His Word.

But then God said: "And I have also given thee that which thou hast not asked, both riches, and honour: so that there shall not be any among the kings like unto thee all thy days" (1 Kings 3:13).

You see, Solomon had an upright heart and asked for wisdom so he would be a just ruler over God's people. He desired to manage well. And because he didn't ask for money, God indeed blessed him with a lot of it. God will never give you more than you can handle.

So, when it comes to giving in general, and certainly giving an offering, God looks at the heart. Give your offerings with no expectation of receiving anything in return, and watch the Lord's faithfulness bloom right before your eyes as you obediently live at the INTERSECTION of God's Wealth and God's Wisdom.

Obedience in Support

Your local church has many callings: building community centers, feeding the poor, teaching the youth, supporting widows, single mothers and military spouses ... the list goes on and on. One reason you care for your home church is because you respect the purpose they fulfill.

If you are always squirming when the offering basket comes around, you may need to check your attitude. You might need to, as Zig Ziglar famously said, get a checkup from the neck up.

The church may not always make decisions you agree with, but you don't know everything that is going on behind the scenes. If you don't trust your pastors or staff, and it is for a valid reason, you should pray that God would speak to you about these feelings. You should not be in a position where you are mentally and spiritually at odds with your home church.

This dilemma is too important to skip. Find a church you have no major issues with and therefore have no hesitation in supporting. But if you have been hopping from church to church for many months and can't find a "fit," the problem may not be the churches you are visiting; the issue may be you.

Pray and seek wise counsel. You need a church home. I mention in *Biblical Faith Meets Financial Strategy*, Chapter 3: the church is imperfect because it is full of imperfect people, but it is vital for your growth and the wellbeing of the community it serves.

Why? Because God said so.

Paul writes to the Church at Corinth: "Upon the first day of the week let every one of you lay by him in store, as God hath prospered him, that there be no gatherings when I come" (1 Corinthians 16:2). In other words, God has allowed you to prosper, so set aside a portion you want to give out of thanksgiving and have it ready for church on Sunday.

In 1 Corinthians chapter 9, Paul also mentions how it is right for you to support the pastor and those who bring the gospel. There must have been members of this church who didn't understand the needs of their pastors. So Paul references scripture in Deuteronomy to make it clear.

"For it is written in the law of Moses, Thou shalt not muzzle the mouth of the ox that treadeth out the corn. Doth God take care for oxen?" (1 Corinthians 9:9) Many pastors today are being "muzzled" and are not being compensated fittingly. I know there may be those who point to the few rotten apples in the bunch.

First, there are exceptionally few corrupt pastors who are being paid excessive salaries or robbing the church. The media only promotes and exaggerates the occasional terrible story.

Second, if you see that going on at your church, that is very much a reason to leave. From my research, most pastors are not getting rich by any means. So, find a wholesome home church, return the tithe, and support them with your offerings as you are able.

Missionaries depend on God's sustenance for all their efforts. And He does. God could do His work without our generosity; remember, He owns everything. But God gives us the privilege to take part in His work and His blessing. That is why missionaries are supported through your offerings and pledges to them.

In an article outlining *The Right Perspective on Supporting Missions*, Bible.org gives five points to consider:

1. *Our Giving to Missions Must Continually Be Renewed*
2. *Our Giving to Missions Should Be a Ministry of Great Joy*
3. *Our Giving to Missions Is Needed but Not Necessary*
4. *Our Giving to Missions Should Be Intentional*
5. *Our Giving to Missions Is Honored by God* [2]

Are you supposed to give to every ministry raising funds? Of course not. Do your own research to learn more about giving into the mission field, and then pray about ways you can give in this special way. Ask God what ministry, how, when, and how much. He will help you plan a strategy to go along with the wealth He has placed in your possession.

While in the Navy, I was a part of a trip to an elementary school in Guam where they needed a team to come help with repairs and restoration to their building. As I painted the pillars outside, I met people from different walks of life and could share my story with them. The day ended with an event where the children came out and performed dances and told us how much they appreciated us. Once again, I (the giver) got so much out of this experience that I was not expecting or doing it for. The only thing I gave up was time and energy, but I received so much more than I'd spent.

Most people will never have the opportunity to travel to dreadfully impoverished and remote places on earth, but we can all give finances and other resources to those in desperate need. There are also local missionaries going into the prisons, the homeless shelters, the nursing homes, and the universities to preach the Gospel.

You will not find a shortage of opportunities to support. However, many of them have discovered a lack of people who support them. Too many go under-funded because of our disobedience.

In the last chapter of *God's Ownership Meets Money Management*, I mentioned how our Father wants us not to steal and covet as the world does. There would be no place for greed if everyone would only obey. As Paul said, "If you are a thief, quit stealing. Instead, use your hands for good hard work, and then **give generously to others in need**" (Ephesians 4:28 NLT).

To Honor and Worship the Lord Your God

What better reason to give than to honor and worship the Lord your God? Did you know that giving is a form of worship? Notice I said, "Your God," not "My God," or "The God." We have the same God, but this is a personal relationship. The act of giving honor and worship to Your God is an intimate and personal moment.

In the Old Testament, offerings were often burnt offerings, meaning, animal sacrifices on the altar. These sacrifices were an integral part of worship. Mark Roberts writes in an article for Church Leaders: "Though the Israelites sang songs and prayed prayers, the core of their worship was offering sacrifices and gifts in the temple in Jerusalem. Giving tangible offerings was a way for people to express their devotion to the Lord. Such worship was costly, requiring that people give up valuable animals, produce, coinage, and precious metals."[3]

You will read many times that God says these offerings are a "sweet-smelling sacrifice that is acceptable to God and pleases Him." Your offerings are still a satisfying aroma unto the Lord, even though they are not burnt sacrifices.

Paul writes to the church in Philipi after collecting the offering that had been set aside, "But I have all, and abound: I am full, having received of Epaphroditus the things which were sent from you, an odour of a sweet smell, a sacrifice acceptable, wellpleasing to God" (Philippians 4:18).

We show God reverence and honor when we choose to give to Him, His church, and His under-shepherds rather than do something else with those resources. God knows you have given up something when you give. He understands your opportunity cost.

Jesus is the chief teacher of all, and He taught about money a lot. In fact, He spoke about money more than love. I think that is because your heart is where you put your treasure.

While teaching His disciples about appropriate giving to the church, He uses a moment where they are at the temple, watching people as they bring their offerings. He points out how a rich man gave a large sum of money and made a show of his giving. Here Jesus was pointing out the state of his heart, not that he was rich.

But there was a poor widow who gave just a small amount. Then Jesus says, "Verily I say unto you, That this poor widow hath cast more in, than all they which have cast into the treasury: For all they did cast in of their abundance; but she of her want did cast in all that she had, even all her living" (Mark 12:43-44).

She was giving out of worship and thanksgiving. Her offering was honoring to the Lord. If your offering is not everything from the depths of your soul, God wants nothing. God desires your heart, not your money.

"Then the people rejoiced, for that they offered willingly, because with perfect heart they offered willingly to the Lord: and David the king also rejoiced with great joy" (1 Chronicles 29:9).

King David is a man of worship; as you know, he wrote most of the book of Psalm. His prayer of adoration concerning the offering collected to build the temple is recorded here in Chronicles.

"O our God, we thank you and praise your glorious name! But who am I, and who are my people, that we could give anything to you? Everything we have has come from you, and we give you only what you first gave us! ... O Lord our God, even this material we have gathered to build a Temple to honor your holy name comes from you! It all belongs to you! I know, my God, that you examine our hearts and rejoice when you find integrity there. You know I have done all this with good motives, and I have watched your people offer their gifts willingly and joyously" (1 Chronicles 29:13-14,16-17 NLT).

That's the way to worship the Lord with your offerings! I want to have a heart like David when I give. Each time I put something in the offering basket, I intentionally take a moment to pray. Not the verbatim prayer that the person in the pulpit spoke before they took up the offering. I mean a special prayer. It's a conversation between me and my Master, who is my King and my Savior. I will not tell you what I pray; and in fact, it's different every time. You

Generosity is

not an excuse to

borrow money.

need to give and pray specifically in the moment, that intimate moment between you and Your God.

Giving is worship. We know God owns everything; we know He doesn't need our money, for it is not ours, it's His. But when we give from the prosperity He has given us, we are saying, "Thank You; we love You; we worship You."

The Seriouseness of a Pledge

Keeping your word is brilliant advice for every aspect of your life, especially in your financial life. All banking institutions, mortgage companies, utilities, creditors and billers want the same thing from each of their customers: pay as agreed. This means paying on time for the amount you promised.

For an offering, though, it gets even more serious. It is important to never pressure yourself or be forced into giving because, once you've made that commitment to God, you need to fulfill that gift.

Numbers 30:2 says, "If a man vows a vow to the Lord, or swears an oath to bind himself by a pledge, he shall not break his word. He shall do according to all that proceeds out of his mouth" (ESV).

When my wife and I were in a ton of debt, we reacted to a pledge for a church building project with no prayer. This is called letting the flesh lead as opposed to the Spirit. I felt we should do a certain amount because it was the amount that someone else had pledged. We certainly could have afforded it with our income, but we also had a debt to pay.

Little did I know that the Holy Spirit would come with a reproof later that month. If you have read *Biblical Faith Meets Financial Strategy*, you'd remember the Financial Guidance from the Holy Spirit I presented. Don't forget those truths because they will keep you centered on the will of God and keep you out of hot water.

We were convicted to stop being a slave to the lender and only be a slave to Christ. God was leading us out of debt, so we could help many others do the same. The Lord wanted us to commit all income after tithe, taxes, and our basic necessities to demolishing our debt. But I had committed to this project—I had made a pledge.

Generosity is not an excuse to borrow money. It might seem noble and righteous, but when you give money in a financial state where you cannot afford to, you are not being a good steward. Specifically, when you owe money to lenders or other people, you must focus on removing that burden of financial slavery. You are in effect borrowing money to give when you choose to give over paying off your obligations.

I asked God what we could do to get out of our commitment, and I received no response. So I began searching the scripture and found the answer. Sometimes the answer to prayer is there in black and white in the Bible, and in my case, I should have known better. Our rash vow was not the will of God, and now I can teach others by my testimony.

Jesus has some advice for us on this matter: "Again you have heard that it was said to those of old, 'You shall not swear falsely, but shall perform to the Lord what you have sworn.' But I say to you, Do not take an oath at all, either by heaven, for it is the throne of God, or by the earth, for it is his footstool, or by Jerusalem, for it is the city of the great King. And do not take an oath by your head, for you cannot make one hair white or black. **Let what you say be simply 'Yes' or 'No'; anything more than this comes from evil**" (Matthew 5:33-37 ESV).

Never renege on your commitment.

If we had not made that pledge, we would have gotten out of debt even faster, freeing us to give even more after debt freedom.

You never know what the future holds; therefore a vow could easily lead to a predicament. Sometimes God has a plan for resources that have been impulsively pledged elsewhere. Other times there may be hard times around the corner, which could have been far less worse if those funds had not be sworn to be given away.

Our financial management decisions are very short-sighted because we can't see past the situation right before our eyes. But the Lord sees far down the road and can guide us if only we would ask. There will be times that God prompts you to make a pledge; only make sure it is His plan and not your hasty plan.

Again, a moment of impatience came over me. I was tempted to jump to the prompting of the Holy Spirit and begin attacking the debt with no regard to the pledge I had made. Essentially, because of my first mistake, I was going to allow the pledged amount to be at the bottom of the list of obligations, making a grave error. Never give God your leftovers.

The prophet Malachi warns against this in the days when most offerings were animals.

> *"Think of it! Animals that are stolen and crippled and sick are being presented as offerings! Should I accept from you such offerings as these?"* *asks the Lord. "Cursed is the cheat who promises to give a fine ram from his flock but then sacrifices a defective one to the Lord. For I am a great king," says the Lord of Heaven's Armies, "and my name is feared among the nations!" (Malachi 1:13b-14 NLT)*

I almost ended up allowing the entire plan to go from bad to worse, but the Word of God never returns void. Placing the pledge at the top of the list was the right thing to do. We put a plan together to pay the pledge as promised first; then obediently take care of every other debt. Then we presented it to the Lord, asking for His guidance and help along the way.

It wasn't a perfect journey, for we wandered off to do things our own way a few times. But by the grace of God, He expedited the plan. We learned a lot, grew closer in our relationships with Christ, and became much more efficient in our money management. Learn from our story; you can grow in your intimacy with the King of kings without the painful lessons.

Planning to be generous is a must, but making sure it is in line with God's will for your divine provision is critically important.

Part II

Give Much Without
Spending Much Money

CHAPTER FOUR

No Shame in Not Giving

"The Spirit of the Sovereign Lord is upon me, for the Lord has anointed me to bring good news to the poor. He has sent me to comfort the brokenhearted and to proclaim that captives will be released and prisoners will be freed" (Isaiah 61:1 NLT).

Sometimes you will not be able to find room in the budget to spend money on someone on an occasion. Do not let these moments result in shame. I will show you ways you can give big without spending much money. But before you can do that with the right motive and

You must be

honest with yourself,

be honest with others,

not make it a

competition, and give

for the right reasons.

conscience, you need to understand that God sees your heart's desires.

Also know that you will not always be in your current situation. Giving too much now will ruin the potential of your future generosity. There are people who give more than they can afford today, which puts a strain on their giving tomorrow, and even more strain on the next occurrence; it never ends. I've seen this far too often, and it is difficult to break the cycle of giving beyond your means.

Remember how you shouldn't feel pressure to give when considering an offering? Well, the same goes for giving gifts for birthdays, anniversaries, holidays, and beyond. The main reason people feel pressure in these moments is because they are more concerned about what other people will think instead of what the Lord of All would have you do.

I know, we want others to like us, but I assure you that gift-giving should not be the driver for being appreciated and loved. If someone or some organization will only value you if you give a certain way, that situation is toxic. Move on and feel no indignity.

"There is good news," says the Lord in Isaiah 61:1 speaking to the people of Israel. As a child of God, I claim these promises for myself. Read this entire chapter where Jesus proclaims His promises to those who feel ashamed of their current state of wealth and possessions. In fact, there will be rejoicing for God's Provision is more than enough.

"Instead of shame and dishonor, you will enjoy a double share of honor. You will possess a double portion of prosperity in your land, and everlasting joy will be yours" (Isaiah 61:7 NLT).

These next four sections will walk you through some things to consider concerning gift-giving when you don't have much money to spend. Even when you do have money, there are opportunity costs, which I wrote about in Chapter 6 of *Biblical Faith Meets Financial Strategy*.

So, you must be honest with yourself, be honest with others, not make it a competition, and give for the right reasons.

Be Honest With Yourself

Strategic money management happens when you are honest with yourself. You must know at what stage you are at on your financial journey and where the limits are. Read the "Be Happy" section in *Biblical Faith Meets Financial Strategy*. Healthy boundaries are a must for financial success.

"He who walks blamelessly and does what is right and speaks truth in his heart" (Psalm 15:2 ESV).

When King David used the phrase "speaks truth in his heart," he is saying to be honest with yourself. This is vital in doing what is right.

During my family's wake-up call and process of debt demolition, we had to say no to ourselves. One of those areas was saying no to buying gifts for everyone for every reason. We are natural givers, so we didn't want to stop giving all the time. Sometimes saying no to yourself stings, and this was one of those times for us.

But we had to be honest with ourselves. We had to sit down and plan how we would be good stewards with God's money, not just for today or next week, but long term. Everything we do today has a reverberating effect on our financial trajectory.

Just think back to a time a year ago or more when you made a significant financial decision, whether it was a wise purchase or excellent investment or meeting a big savings goal. How has that decision affected your standing today?

Then try the same exercise from the other perspective. Think about that awful choice you made with money years ago, that horrible purchase or poor investment or money wasted you should have saved. How has that choice impacted your current pocketbook position?

Then I remembered opportunity cost. For every penny I use for gifts, what am I giving up? In our case, it would take us longer to get out of the hole we had dug if we kept spending at the same clip. We had to be honest and do what we knew we needed to accomplish for our goals to come to fruition.

You can, of course, run a scenario like this for any decision. For example, you could put the $1000 of

Christmas gifts you are buying this year into a retirement calculator to see what that same $1000 could grow to 40 years from now. If you do it, you may never give a gift again—just kidding!

But really, giving may very well outweigh the other choices you have with the same amount of money. Blessing others is one of the most valuable objectives you will ever have. But sometimes, you must be honest with yourself and say no, so you don't miss the path you should have followed.

Once we laid out a five-year forecast and ran several scenarios, the choice we needed to make became glaringly apparent. We could keep giving and spending like we always had and be debt-free in five years, all the while not giving to everyone and every cause we wanted to bless. Or we could offer nothing that costs us financially for two years, focusing all our disposable Inflow on the goal, after which we could give as we had always wanted to and more.

Looking back, those two years went by faster than we thought. When you are in the middle of a mess, it seems like you will never get out. But in the end, it feels like a moment in time.

Also, we did not know at the beginning of the journey that our son would get married four years later. If we had taken the slow and lame five year route, it would have been a struggle to help with the wedding. But because we "sacrificed" for a couple of years, we could give the amount we wanted to with no strain. I'm so glad God led us to the better choice.

We would not have enjoyed the right choice of being responsible and taking care of cleaning up our mess if we had not been honest with ourselves. Don't get me wrong; it took lots of prayer and courage to make the right choice. It doesn't feel so great initially, but you are glad you didn't fall for the lie once you come out on the other side.

By the way, in the Zero In Financial blog target: Demolish Debt, you will find several posts for helping you with the mindset around debt. You will find the logic behind getting out of debt before being financially generous or any other extra spending. So, if you owe anyone for any reason, give those posts a read and let me know if you need guidance.[1]

Be Honest With Others

The next step is to be honest with others. As I said before, I've seen so many situations where there is pressure to give gifts. This burden may stem from your parents, in-laws, friends, co-workers, church … the list goes on and on.

They may mean well, but they are not the stewards of the resources you have been tasked with managing. They will not stand before God and recount the job you did. And you will not be responsible for their decisions either.

I must warn you: this could get toxic. A situation where someone will not talk to you because they didn't get a gift from you on a particular occasion is unhealthy. When your gift to someone else dictates another family member's mood or attitude, watch out! These settings are not acceptable and need to be acknowledged.

You don't need to explain why or why not you are giving a gift to anyone. There is no obligation. But out of courtesy, you may let the other people involved know what your budget is. If you can contribute only $25 for a wedding reception, that is your limit. You have already been honest with yourself; now you are staying open with them.

Here is how the Apostle Paul put it when writing to the church in Corinth:

> *Let the eagerness you showed in the beginning be matched now by your giving. Give in proportion to what you have. Whatever you give is acceptable if you give it eagerly. And give according to what you have, not what you don't have. Of course, I don't mean your giving should make life easy for others and hard for yourselves. I only mean that there should be some equality. Right now you have plenty and can help those who are in need. Later, they will have plenty and can share with you when you need it. In this way, things will be equal. As the Scriptures say, "Those who gathered a lot had*

nothing left over, and those who gathered only a little had enough" (2 Corinthians 8:11b-15 NLT).

You should not be strong-armed into giving. If there is a great expectation for you to give a gift to a particular person for a holiday, explain to them that you cannot share this year. Tell them you will be able to in future years once you have taken care of other obligations. This gesture is only a courtesy and is not a requirement for doing the right thing.

Situations in which you feel obligated to give are traps. Don't fall for them. Have no guilt in not going to someone's destination wedding, or feeling as if you must give Mom a gift on Mother's Day, or that Christmas will be ruined if you don't give a gift to your kids. If your loved ones don't understand your current situation, goals, and ultimate financial destination, are they really your loved ones? (Also, you don't really owe them an explanation either.) Let God lead your generosity, not peer, family or social pressure.

Sometimes in the church setting, we may want to match what someone else gives or help meet the presented goal. That is a wonderful gesture, but is it God's will in your life for this opportunity at this moment?

In all giving situations, no matter in church or at home, make prayer your first instinct and wait on the Lord for His direction. The Holy Spirit will keep you from making many erroneous decisions that seem good from a shortsighted perspective. Then you can share with that organization or person where you are at, and what you can honestly contribute.

In the next section, I will look at the many ways you can give a lot without spending much money at all. So don't feel bad if your plan dictates you cannot spend a bunch of cash. As you will see, the church or nonprofit organization you are giving to may appreciate these more valuable gifts far more than a thoughtless check. And the people who are celebrating their special day have many needs and will thank you for being so thoughtful once they see you thinking outside the gift box.

It's Not a Competition

When you find yourself in a poisonous family situation where individuals are complaining, pouting, or even whining about gifts received or not, you should gracefully step away. Unfortunately, this may have been learned and not corrected when we were young children.

Remember when you and your brother or sister fought over the Christmas gift the other one received? Yes, this is a teaching moment that, if not taught, was a missed opportunity. For example, being thankful, appreciative, and grateful for all that God has provided—and loving your sibling enough to share always. And jealousy and envy have no place in this home or in your life.

We needed to discover these principles early because we have a much more difficult time learning these social lessons later in life. And these behaviors are even more embedded in our mentality when we observed our parents acting this way consistently.

Giving is not a competition, so don't fall into the trap. If you are in the store contemplating what gift to get in light of what other people may give the same person, stop yourself. Generosity from the heart means thinking about what the person receiving will enjoy or what will be beneficial. Putting thought into gift-giving is a lost art. Giving out of genuine love is becoming rare.

In an article in the Huffington Post, Brittany Wong quotes Kurt Smith, a therapist in Roseville, California: "Many people turn gift-giving into a measurement of their success and value, rather than what it's supposed to be, which is an expression of love and gratitude. When this happens, gift-giving becomes a recipe for disaster."

She then lists four signs that gift-giving has become toxic:

1. *You buy presents based on how Instagram-worthy they are.*

2. *You get anxious when you think about holiday shopping.*

3. *Your relatives are taken aback by your gifts or embarrassed they didn't get you something as pricey.*[2]

4. *Someone in your family has experienced a financial setback, but your gift-giving plans remain the same.*

Another attitude to avoid is almost being envious of the gift you are giving. This phenomenon seemed strange to me initially, but then I realized that I'd done it after thinking about it. You may remember when you were in the store buying an electronic device for a family member; then suddenly you get the thought, "I want one too."

It happens—squash it when it does. Remember who you are loving. When you have properly budgeted for the month, you may have planned enough to buy that person that gift and, at the same time, an adequate amount in the corresponding budget category to buy yourself one as well.

If buying that gift is bothering you because she will have one and you will not, you need to leave the store, click away from that website, or close that shopping app. Pray that God will help you give with the right attitude and not just know in your head, but know in your spirit that it is more blessed to give than receive.

Right in the middle of Jesus' sermon on the mount, He warns, "Take heed that ye do not your alms before men, to be seen of them: otherwise ye have no reward of your Father which is in heaven" (Matthew 6:1). Alms is traditional money given to the poor, but I believe this can apply to all gifts.

Jesus was responding to those who wanted to give so that others would praise and see them. Jesus warns that your gift in heaven may be at stake.

Give For the Right Reasons

Giving for the right reasons is the only way to give. But I must point out some of the bothersome trends that are happening around gift-giving today.

Okay, this is just my opinion, but I have to say it. Gift cards are not thoughtful. Even if you get your mother a gift card to her favorite store, you have put forth minimal effort in getting that gift, and to me, it seems kind of lazy.

I understand that sometimes a gift card may be appropriate, like for your client or someone who provides a service to you. But even then, you could do better. I would suggest that some of the gift ideas in the following section—which cost you no money—would be more sentimental or meaningful than a gift card.

Thank you for letting me get that off my chest.

So, there are many right reasons to give. First, to display the character of Christ, the Creator of everything, and Master Giver. When you give to people, especially outside your family, you open up the opportunity to share the love of Christ with them.

Second, you give to fulfill a need in that person's life. There are specific seasons when we give more often than other times, but anytime is the best time to meet someone's needs. I mentioned how awesome it feels to be generous, and these times are some of the most emotionally rewarding. In fact, when I receive a gift at an unexpected moment, it almost adds another layer of appreciation to that surprise.

Third, give to celebrate someone's milestone or success. This individual or group is the reason for the celebration, not you. She graduated. He turned twenty-one. They got married. Celebrations are breeding grounds for those ugly sentiments I mentioned earlier. Jealousy abounds. But you must be the light and show others what the love of Christ does through a person's life.

Of course the commercialization of Christmas has gone too far. I'm not mad at gift-giving at Christmas time; the problem is that the tradition of giving gifts has overshadowed the Gift of gifts, Jesus. You want to bless others for the right reason, and I think we need to make sure the recipient knows why they are receiving a particular holiday gift.

Talk about what happened over 2000 years ago that changed the world. Have conversations about what happened two years ago when you accepted Jesus into your life. The Christmas season is the best time to give the gift of joy, peace, and a story that can change their lives.

Instead of sending the mass-produced pictures of your family sitting on the beach, why not send a personalized hand-written note with the story of Jesus' impact on your family and how He can impact theirs?

When it comes to giving for the right reason, you can be sure God wants you to give and provide a way for you to give. "He will always make you rich enough to be generous at all times, so that many will thank God for your gifts which they receive from us" (2 Corinthians 9:11 GNT).

In this passage of scripture, you see He will always make you rich, but riches are not always monetary. You will be rich in experience, knowledge, talent, and other things, and we should "be generous at all times" with these resources. All times? Yes. A very valid reason to give is "just because". That may be the best time to give indeed.

This idea leads me to some of the best gifts you can give, and none of them requires the use of your debit card, checkbook, or piggy bank.

CHAPTER FIVE

Give Without
Spending a Penny

I first started writing blog posts about giving without spending a penny for those I coached in the middle of their debt demolition plan. When you are Demolishing Debt, you have no room to spend money on anything that is not 100% essential.

Also, there are many people that I coach who have big goals they want to achieve. For example, putting up cash for the adoption of a child can take a lot of resources. The best way to tackle those massive goals is to concentrate on as much of your Inflow as you can. You will still save for retirement or college funds, for example. But all other Outgo needs to be focused on the task at hand!

Speaking of college funding, this is another area that may require high amounts of cash in a short time. For example, you have a sixteen-year-old who is planning to go to a local college, but you realize that you haven't saved up a penny towards that goal. Of course, you could and should have her work a part-time job and apply for scores of scholarships and grants; but you also want to make sure you cash flow the entire four years. That is going to require a lot of catch up, so for a couple years it would be wise to hone your resources for the big hairy audacious goal at hand.

Another time you may maximize this strategy is when you are in the midst of an emergency. If there is a season of income loss or hospitalization or major repair, you may just want to press pause on the big gift spending during this time. This is a key part of Optimizing Outgo, where you move money from certain budget categories to handle an increase in others.

Notice I said, "press pause." This is only a season. And it too shall pass. But after you see how big you can give without spending a penny, you may never go back.

So, what happens when it is your best friends baby shower? What about your grandmother's seventy-fifth birthday? How do you handle the Christmas season coming up when you have little ones looking for plastic stuff under the tree?

Well, no one would die if you didn't give anything as we discovered in the last chapter. But there is a way to give that we many times miss. This has helped many who find themselves in a tight budgeting situation.

But then I began to see how giving without spending a penny has helped those who don't fall into this predicament. You may just want to provide extraordinary gifts. God has given you an abundance of resources which go far beyond monetary sources. He wants you to use them to bless others.

These gifts show extreme generosity and love and just so happen to cost no money. These gifts are some of the most valuable and most appreciated gifts that one can ever give. As they are far more common than in years past, I believe now more than ever before, we should return to the gifts of Time, Hospitality, and Talent.

How to Give Time

There is nothing more valuable than love, and not too far behind love is time. They go hand in hand. When you love someone, it is so easy to give up your time for them.

Time is priceless because of its scarcity. Everyone has the same amount, twenty-four hours per day, and what you don't spend you can't take with you. Oh, how I wish you could get rollover minutes!

Someone once said: "Yesterday is history. Tomorrow a mystery. Today is a gift. That's why it's called the present!"

Think of it this way. You could *spend time* at the department store searching for the perfect gift, standing in long lines, only to spend a bunch of money on something they may not value a whole lot. Or you could *spend time* serving and loving them, which they will appreciate far more.

Friends and family may take your time for granted. But even in that case, you can do something above and beyond that will blow them away.

For instance, if you go over to your brother's house and spend time with him and his family all the time, you may think that giving the gift of time would not mean much to him. But what if you told him you were coming over to do a deep spring cleaning of his house for his birthday? Or you washed his car without him knowing before he woke up to it sparkling. Maybe you cook for the whole family with their food, in their kitchen, but saving them time by spending yours.

I remember making paper coupons for my wedding anniversary. You have probably seen something like this before. Each voucher can be "cashed in" as needed. They say things like, "I will draw you a bubble bath and make your favorite tea," or "I'll cook dinner and do all the dishes." They could offer the silliest of things, but they mean a lot because they are personal. And of course, each of them requires you to spend your most valuable commodity—time.

"As we have therefore opportunity, let us do good unto all men, especially unto them who are of the household of faith" (Galatians 6:10).

You may know someone for whom you would like to give up some time so they could gain some time! For example, you see your neighbor doesn't have a car and commutes to work two hours each way by bus. So, you see her walking to the bus stop and let her know you can take her to work and pick her up each day. No charge, just a no strings attached gift. You have saved her possibly three hours a day, which maybe costs you an extra fifteen minutes per day.

Time is of the utmost value when giving to a charity or non-profit organization. There are so many opportunities to give back to your community or a cause you believe in by giving up a Saturday. You could clean up the recreation center, rake and mow the lawn, paint the church gym, and on and on.

Volunteering is truly an act of generosity. Who cares if it is not "tax deductible"? If you are only giving to charities that allow you to write it off, that's not the right reason.

Instead of your family giving each other gifts this Christmas, you could try going to the local food bank or soup kitchen and serve the homeless. You will come back with more joy than you would have had by receiving plastic stuff. Your family will remember that holiday for many years to come.

We parents spend far too little time with our children in intimate settings regularly. What happened to reading a story to them at bedtime, or spending time exploring the woods, playing catch, or building a snowman? Those gifts are priceless memories that will last forever.

But for a more unique occasion, you can give your kids a gift of time where you spend a whole day doing whatever they want with the stuff they already have. I'm sure there is something that has been collecting dust in their closet. They may come up with some ideas that will challenge you, make you do some research, or physically tire you out. Your kids will have a blast, and you will grow closer than ever. It will be worth it, and you will both be blessed beyond belief.

Time is far more valuable than money and is appreciated many times more than material things. I heard someone once say, "When we can see our time through the eyes of opportunity and not see it as a limitation, there's no ceiling to what God can accomplish through us."

How to Give Hospitality

Oh, the college days, when I had little money, plenty of debt, and ambitions as far as the sky. I can remember the good times and the not-so-good times. But what I most remember are the meals and the fellowship when someone would invite the broke college kid over to their home.

Hospitality is a godsend to many people. A homeless person in need of a meal, the military service member who is far away from family, a single parent barely making it, the senior citizen with no relatives nearby and, yes, the broke college kid. The warmth of a home and that home-cooked meal goes a long way.

As Nehemiah said to the people, "'Go and celebrate with a feast of rich foods and sweet drinks, and **share gifts of food with people who have nothing prepared.** This is a sacred day before our Lord. Don't be dejected and sad, for the joy of the Lord is your strength!' ... So the people went away to eat and drink at a festive meal, to **share gifts of food, and to celebrate with great joy** because they had heard God's words and understood them" (Nehemiah 8:10,12 NLT).

No gadget, game, or gift card can compare to the company of people who want to talk and enjoy your presence. That day of laughter and singing will be etched in the recipient's memory for years to come. They may even pay it forward when they are in your position. Don't miss this opportunity to give to those who need it most.

There was an oft forgotten wealthy woman in the Bible who understood this power of hospitality.

> *And it fell on a day, that Elisha passed to*
> *Shunem, where was a great woman; and she*
> *constrained him to eat bread. And so it was, that*
> *as oft as he passed by, he turned in thither to eat*

> *bread. And she said unto her husband, Behold*
> *now, I perceive that this is an holy man of God,*
> *which passeth by us continually. Let us make a*
> *little chamber, I pray thee, on the wall; and let us*
> *set for him there a bed, and a table, and a stool,*
> *and a candlestick: and it shall be, when he cometh*
> *to us, that he shall turn in thither (2 Kings*
> *4:8-10).*

Elisha, the prophet, had little money. He depended on the generosity of offerings and people like this woman of Shunem. She took the burden off his shoulders to find a place to stay when he was in town. Room and board, free of charge.

I suppose this woman could have just given him a bunch of money and sent him off to a hotel. But this gave Elisha the comfort of a home away from home. She set up a room just for him, so he could make it his own.

You may have had money, but you can give hospitality with no extra cost at all. Do you have a spare room or two that you could set up for a missionary to lay their head? How about just inviting a traveling evangelist over for a meal?

Try giving a different kind of wedding gift. You could surprise your friend with a gift of hospitality. If there are people in the wedding party who are coming from out of town and need a place to stay, you may be able to provide. That spare bed may just turn out to be a blessing and save them a couple hundred dollars in hotel costs. That will be a far better gift than a third toaster.

This experience may very well help you grow as a person as well. I know you may think how you don't want to have someone stay in your house because you are particular and don't want them to mess things up. Well, they must have had issues in this area during the days of the first church as well. Peter wrote, "Offer hospitality to one another without grumbling" (1 Peter 4:9 NIV).

I've mentioned having someone come to your home to share a meal. This rarely costs any additional money for we waste so much food—at least in America. Cooking yields several servings and to add a plate most likely won't require more ingredients.

My wife and I are now empty-nesters, and she always says it is difficult to cook for two. When she creates a meal, there are a good bit of leftovers. I love to enjoy her creation again for lunch a day or two later, but what if we could serve and give to those who would appreciate a hot meal with a side of company?

I began thinking about how we don't think of doing something special for the first responders, teachers, and veterans that go to our church. I need to make a list and check it twice, and this list is not to get (like the one for Santa Claus) but to give.

How to Give Talent

I cannot believe some of the unique creations I have received from people. Everyone has such distinctive and extraordinary talents, and many times they never think of it as something they can give. You may think your skill is not that big of a deal. But to someone else, it would be a cherished gift.

You musicians: record an original song that you wrote just for them. If you have the talent of dancing, record a short video with a custom-tailored performance. Artists: paint or draw a unique piece with their name in their favorite colors. Crafters: knitting, necklaces, bracelets, etc. (whatever your specialty), with unique patterns representing their hobbies or favorite pastimes.

Writers can create poetry or short stories. Your spouse or children would cherish a journal you have been writing for them over the last twelve weeks or twelve months. Imagine you give your daughter, turning eighteen, a memoir of short writings from the previous 365 days about how much she means to you.

Whatever you do, do it to celebrate their character. Make something that expresses the recipient's personality and is unique and specific to them. This gift never lets them down because they see your love for them in it immediately. Plus, it is not a cookie cutter gift. It is as unique as they are.

The best gifts I have ever received are in this category. I realize the time it took to create the present. The giver's talent is on display. And the love is overwhelmingly clear.

I've seen this used for charity as well. The most touching example was an elderly lady that had the gift of knitting. Her daughter's Navy command was on deployment during Christmas, and she made hats and scarves for every sailor deployed on the ship. There were symbols of their vessel, deployment dates, special wishes and prayers, and so on, sewn on each one. They were so appreciated; everyone kept them for many years to come. She had the materials donated to her, so she didn't have to spend a penny.

Some people can take a piece of scrap wood and create works of art. I am amazed at their beautiful creations, as are all the people who receive their gifts. They have the tools; the materials are free; but the time they spend is priceless. The same goes for crafters of metal, clay, and leather.

What about you educators with the talent of teaching? If you know of a struggling single mom with a kid having difficulty in a subject, you can give the gift of free tutoring. It will be a load off her plate plus pay dividends when her child's grades are high enough to get the scholarship he needs. That's the gift that keeps on giving.

Churches and charity need volunteers with specific talents. People skilled in carpentry, sewing, and artistic

You may think

your skill is

not that big of a deal.

But to someone else,

it would be a

cherished gift.

painting are in high demand. Also, if you have the talent for teaching children, that would be greatly appreciated.

God gave you whatever talents you possess. It's time for you to use them for others, giving God the glory all the way. You see this with people throughout the Bible, including Bezaleel, whose workmanship went into the Tabernacle materials:

> *And I have filled him with the spirit of God, in wisdom, and in understanding, and in knowledge, and in all manner of workmanship, To devise cunning works, to work in gold, and in silver, and in brass, And in cutting of stones, to set them, and in carving of timber, to work in all manner of workmanship (Exodus 31:3-5).*

Don't say you have no talent, for everyone has a special gift. Teach someone how to play an instrument, cook, make a computer program, or do an exercise routine. You may specialize in calligraphy or skateboarding or gardening, or Lego building.

Just because I may not have mentioned your talent, it doesn't mean you have nothing to give. Think about when your friends say, "Wow, you are so good at that!" or "How did you do that?" Those are clues to your untapped gifts.

Betty, the blogger behind AllRoundJesus.com writes, "Whatever your gift/talent is, it is unique to you. It may not look like much to you, but rest assured it is not meaningless but useful."[1] So many people would love to receive the gifts only you can provide. Don't forsake the talent God has given you.

These are the Most Cherished Gifts

Don't tell yourself that you don't have something to give. Money is unnecessary most times; you just have to be creative with your time, hospitality, and talent. These are the most cherished gifts and allow you to become more like Jesus.

If you put your mind to it and do some planning, you could make time by cutting out something unnecessary from your day. You may set aside a day of binge-watching your favorite show to give some time to your youth group at church. You could sacrifice one football game to give your wife a surprise at-home date night. There is always time to serve mom and dad on their special days. You may even take in a foster child for a season.

iGiftFund writes in their blog: "Studies show that 65% of Americans donate time to charitable causes, averaging $23 per hour for $173 billion in economic impact. Without volunteers, many of our religious, social, and charitable institutions would be lost. You never know what impact your volunteering will have on your local community or even the world."[2]

The author continues, "Different from volunteering your time, talent giving is volunteering the unique and personal talents you have that others may not. Their value is priceless to the charity that receives it."

So, no matter if you are giving your Friday nights to the Salvation Army or you have a talent for transforming one man's junk into another man's treasured birthday gift, continue giving without spending a penny.

Even if you have the funds to donate or money to give as a graduation gift, consider giving them gifts of time, hospitality, and talent. The recipient will be blown away. These gifts mean so much because that's how God designed our hearts to give and receive.

"As every man hath received the gift, even so minister the same one to another, as good stewards of the manifold grace of God" (1 Peter 4:10).

CHAPTER SIX

Give Without
Spending A Lot

Now that you see how to give ultra-valuable gifts without spending any money at all, let's look at some ways to meet other's needs while spending just a little. These ideas may not be free of charge, but none of them will cost much. I can even see someone who is intensely getting out of debt, or immersed in a big savings goal, doing these with no strain on their budget.

Let me make a personal declaration: I will continue regifting, reusing, and repurposing with no shame! No matter how wealthy I get, I will always use these strategies to recycle stuff that I already own. Why buy new if you can utilize the stuff that is just cluttering up your garage and cupboards? No reason at all.

There is a danger of keeping too much stuff anyway. I've had a problem in the past where I didn't want to throw anything away because of the potential for having a use for it in the future. Don't hoard. Remember, there is a time for everything: "a time to search and a time to give up, a time to keep and a time to throw away" (Ecclesiastes 3:6 NIV).

These strategies won't always work when giving a last-minute gift. You need to think ahead and be ready in someone's time of need. In fact, I've found things in the Summer which happen to be a perfect gift for someone the next Winter.

Furthermore, when buying anything over a certain dollar amount, you should be mindful of that proverbial line in your budget's sand. Bargain shopping can become a sport, and some people really have a lot of fun finding deals. And when you can spend near-zero while getting colossal value, what could be better?

Well, I wanted to find ways I could find new life out of things I already have for little money, so I did my research, aka asking my wife! The good news is that I got a ton of ideas from her. The bad news is that I can't possibly write about all of them, or this chapter would never end. So, I want to present to you my favorite six ideas.

I will present two suggestions from the Reuse category. Then there will be two concepts which require Repurposing. Lastly, I will give you two Regifting ideas.

Check out the INTERSECTION Resource Page[1] for a more exhaustive list. There will be additional suggestions added in the future, so make sure to sign up for updates.

But before I go into this short list, there needs to be some explanation as to why you would want to use this strategy. I don't want you to think that this is a form of being a cheapskate or stingy in your giving strategy. Also, the terms Reuse, Repurpose and Regift could use a bit of defining.

Save Money While Being Generous

I started on this journey to find new ways to give big without breaking the bank. You might ask, "How are you generous when it doesn't cost you much?" Well, you may not know that the receiver of the gift may cherish it in a way that you wouldn't. You may not understand that spending time, energy, and talent to create a gift could "cost" you more than dollars and cents.

We think about price tags too much in our materialistic society today, and we don't think about the person to whom we are giving. The expression, "It's the thought that counts," has little meaning when you haven't put thought into the gift. We'd rather put a tiny bit of thought into an expensive gift—as if that's impressive— than spend a ton of thought and energy into a gift that costs financially very little.

Handmade gifts are many more times appreciated than the expensive store-bought trinket. That's when I realized there is no shame in regifting, reusing, or repurposing when you put thought and heart into the item. On the other hand, don't employ these ideas by throwing something together at the last minute. These have no business being Hail Mary gifts.

Saving money is not something you have to be obsessed with but should be a natural part of your money mindset. Proverbs 6:6-8 speaks about the ant as an example of how to save during one season so that you can spend in another season.

> *Take a lesson from the ants, you lazybones. Learn from their ways and become wise! Though they have no prince or governor or ruler to make them work, they labor hard all summer, gathering food for the winter (NLT).*

You can do the same as the ant when it comes to your generosity.

Before I go into the list, let me define how I am using these three terms.

So, regifting, in its base form, is to take a gift that has been received and give it to someone else. In this case, there was no modification to the item except possibly rewrapping. The perfect time to do this is when the recipient will appreciate the thing much more than you would. They may need it, whereas you did not. It's a win-win!

To reuse is to take something and combine it with something else, making it better. The primary reason reusing is not repurposing is that the original item is still in its original form, but it has been given new life by using it again. The gift may have been otherwise thrown away or discarded. But now it's being loved once again and saving the giver money at the same time.

Repurposing has created an entire industry. You can find many crafters on Etsy making a living by repurposing—that is, making the item different and better. These make fantastic gifts (you may never want to give them away).

All three can overlap:

1. Reuse + Repurpose: here you could reuse something you already had, adding other material, then use it for a totally different purpose. Keep it for yourself or give it away.

2. Reuse + Regift: sometimes you could reuse something that was a gift to you, combining it with something else; then regift it.

3. Repurpose + Regift: or you could also take one of these gifts received, create something else out of it, using the new creation as a gift.

Saving money is not something you have to be obsessed with but should be a natural part of your money mindset.

By combining these ideas with items around your home, the possibilities are endless.

So, here are my favorite six ways to get the most out of regifting, reusing, and repurposing!

Reusing

You could reuse these things for yourself, but I will focus on two ideas for reusing items as part of a gift. The first is the gift bag itself, so this is one of those reuse/regift ideas. Open that gift carefully. Don't ruin that bag. Make sure your name is not still visible anywhere. Your future gift for someone else is going in there!

Here is a funny story and warning: Sometimes you can get a gift bag where someone writes your name and a message on that little tag that comes with it. You rip off the tag and reuse the bag, but forgot to look at the bag, which has the mirror image of the message imprinted on it because of the use of a ball-point pen. Oops.

Reuse Gift Bags

Gift bags have become super popular because who enjoys using wrapping paper? (What a pain!) But they are kind of expensive. Here is the deal: no one cares about the gift bag after they see what is inside. We want it to look pretty, and we are not totally cheapskates, so that garbage bag will not cut it.

When you get a gift in a gift bag, treat it nicely and save it for later. If you get enough presents, you will never need to purchase a gift bag again! This tip is a reuse strategy and not regifting because you must add the gift. But I'm sure you will find the perfect set of mugs hiding in your cupboard to add inside that bag.

I know this is the Reuse section, but you can also make this a Repurpose idea. Yes, you can Repurpose the gift bag as gift paper. I found this idea on TotebagFactory.com:

> *What better way to reuse old gift bags than by having them come full circle and becoming wrapping paper! To do this, simply remove the handles and go to town. This works best with a gift bag made from thin paper. If you find that the material is too plain for your liking, try gluing tiny decorations onto it, such as pompoms.*[2]

Also, this blog post will show you how to repurpose that gift bag in eighteen other ways, including a greeting card.

Reuse Mason Jars

Okay, enough of the simple stuff. How about reusing those twenty giant Mason jars that were sitting in front of those mugs? Where did they all come from, anyway? Oh, spaghetti nights.

My wife loves reusing these to create gift kits. You put a bunch of inexpensive smaller items together that are related and make a themed gift jar. Fill in the gaps inside with shredded colored paper and tie a bow around the lid. Voilà!

Here are some examples:

- Sewing supplies
- Hot chocolate Kit
- Mani-Pedi
- Shaving Kit
- Cookie, Cake, or Brownie Mixes
- Mini-Tool Kit
- Travel-Sized Toiletries
- Assorted Candy
- Candles

There are so many ways you can use this idea. Just make sure the theme matches the person you are giving it to, and it will be one of the most appreciated personalized gifts you could ever give. You could get fancy and add their name to the outside of the jar too!

The treats, tools, and toiletries needed may be purchased at Dollar Tree. My wife has totally turned me on to this bargain store. There are all kinds of terrific items you can use to stuff your stockings and your jars with. *Bonus tip: They have cheap gift bags too, just in case you ran out of used ones. Please don't buy those bags at the gift store, which cost five times more.*

Oh, and after they use the stuff inside the jar, guess what? They have a Mason jar. These vessels are great for water, sweet tea, ice coffee, and more. So, this is like two gifts in one. If they don't need the Mason jar, make sure they know about this Reuse category of gift-giving. They may just use it for their next act of generosity.

Repurposing

Now that your cabinets are empty, we need to move to another room.

I'm not going to lie; I find the repurpose category the most difficult for the advanced skills that are needed. But these are some of the best gifts ever. You may not want to give these away, but remember, the mission is to give. Also, repurposing could be regifting if you are using items gifted to you, but it doesn't have to be.

Have you ever been eyeing some items in your own garage sale and thought, "I can make something out of that"? I know I have. Well, at least I had the vision, maybe not the skill.

Even if you don't know if you can make the perfect gift out of this hunk of junk, what if you just try? Sometimes you can give the slightly imperfect gift, but because it was specifically meant for that special person, it meant the world to them. I've been the happy recipient of such a gift, and it really is the thought that counted.

Repurpose Picture Frames or Furniture

Old picture frames can really be used for many things. For example, you could turn it into a chalkboard for the doodlers in your life. Or a whiteboard for the entrepreneurs with the home office. Even a corkboard could be something they could use. Maybe draw some word art or create a calendar out of it.

The idea is to use that frame that is not useful for pictures anymore. Or perhaps you have some that are an odd size. Well, repurpose them!

You may need to sand it down if it is wood or give it a coat of paint. Use their favorite colors; give it character and a personality they would appreciate. If you have multiple wooden frames, you could combine them, making funky shapes and sizes.

Get creative. Use your imagination and use your favorite Internet search tool. Here are five ideas I found on one site presenting 60 Ways to Reuse Old Picture Frames:

- *Earring Display*
- *Key Holder*
- *Table Organizer*
- *Serving Tray*
- *Mirror* [3]

If you are crafty with wood, there are so many large items you could repurpose into gifts. These are big sized gifts, so you would need to know that someone needs this item before surprising them for sure. Also, you don't need

It is wise not to waste

God's resources.

to have them lying around in your home because you can find this stuff in the dumpster or garage sales all over town.

Ideas include turning an old bookshelf into a small kitchen island, a dresser into a bench, and a desk transformed into two nightstands (my favorite). These are pretty intense projects, but they are all 100x the value of the original furniture. Find this list on Big DIY Idea.com.[4]

Repurpose Old Clothing

Let's turn some of those old worn-out clothes into cherished gifts. For example, you can alter an old pair of jeans into headbands, pillows, placemats, hot pads, picnic blankets, and so on. Okay, this one requires some skills and is entirely out of my league. Many of these ideas have detailed instructions out there on a blog, video, or Pinterest board.

If you know how to sew, this one is for you. Many of these are incredible items I would love to receive as a gift.

- Making pillowcases out of t-shirts
- Creating a scarf out of a holey sweater
- Designing baby clothing out of a dress shirt
- Converting a dress into a shopping bag
- Using any colorful apparel to create fabric flowers to accent outfits

As with all the repurposing ideas, God loves when we are creative. He designed us that way, and we are made in His image. Look how creative He is.

Also, we are to manage His wealth well, as you can read about in *God's Ownership Meets Money Management*. There, in Chapter 9, I mention how it is wise not to waste God's resources. Repurposing is a responsible thing to do, whether you use the end product for yourself or be charitable with it. I mentioned Proverbs 21:20 in that book, but I want to restate it here in another translation.

"There is precious treasure and oil in the house of the wise [who prepare for the future], but a short-sighted and foolish man swallows it up and wastes it" (Proverbs 21:20 AMP).

Regifting

"Then Peter said, Silver and gold have I none; but such as I have give I thee ..." (Acts 3:6a).

Regifting may be the easiest to do, but don't underestimate these gifts. Here are two items I've found that I can many times give away. I'm sure you can think of several other things like these.

Regifting Books

I can't tell you how many times I find a book given to me I've never read and now sits on a shelf collecting dust. Sometime I began to read it, and by page ten I know it is just not for me. Other times, I get multiple copies of the same book! It happens.

So, if you are in this situation, think of all your friends and family. Who would love this book? In my case, I usually have two of the same book, so I have previously enjoyed the book. Now, I can highly recommend the book to someone I know and give away my extra copy. They'd never have to know that I received it as a gift from someone else.

Make it extra special by writing a letter to go along with the book. This doesn't cost you any money; only time and thought. Tell them why you think they will enjoy this book and how it made you think of them.

This is more of a Reuse, but don't forget about cookbooks. There are many times you have a beat up, worn cookbook that someone would absolutely love. I learned cookbooks are one of the few books where appearance does not matter. If you have a cookbook you've never used because you know all the recipes you want out of it or it is not your style of cooking, give it away to someone who would enjoy it.

This may be rare, but my son was going to college and needed a ton of required books, of course. Well, someone knew he was taking the same classes they were in and had all the books he needed. What a splendid gift that saved him hundreds of dollars his freshman year!

Used books make incredible gifts when given to the right person. You get the benefit of decluttering as well.

Regifting Mugs

The other regifting idea is similar but found in the kitchen. Have you ever gone to the deepest part of your kitchen cabinet only to find a mug you never knew you had? You got this one for Christmas five years ago and forgot all about it. If it's a nice mug, how about regifting it?

We all have way too many mugs, and we typically use the same eight or so daily. So, if you have a new vessel in the depths of the cupboard, dust it off, clean it up, place it in a nice box or bag, and regift it! This idea makes me feel best when it is a set of mugs, and I'm giving them as a home warming gift to someone who is just starting off.

Regifting Ideas Galore

There are many other things you can regift. Look around your house for those things that are unopened. I have a friend who knew her best friend had the same shoe size, so when she found several pairs of shoes never worn in the back of her closet, she had the perfect gift.

Some say unopened candles are good to regift. Others say jewelry. And don't forget the novelty gifts (Who gives those, anyway?) But whatever you do, take off the tag, make sure it is unused, wrap it, and make sure it is something the recipient can use, needs, and will benefit from.

Check out the INTERSECTION Resource Page[1] for a more exhaustive list. There will be additional suggestions added in the future, so sign up for updates.

intersection.zeroinfinancial.com

CHAPTER SEVEN

The Greatest Gifts You Could Ever Give

Mastercard's marketing campaign launched in the 90s has been one of the best money making slogans of all time. "There are some things money can't buy. For everything else, there's Mastercard." I'm sure you have heard it many times.

A Marketing Week article states:

> *Mastercard's famous slogan, launched in 1997, immediately caught the public's imagination. Almost before there was such a thing as viral campaigns and Internet memes, people were holding up placards at baseball matches listing the*

prices of various objects and then ending with the word "priceless" to emulate the company's marketing campaign.[1]

Obviously I disagree with their conclusion that "for everything else, there's Mastercard" … cash works just fine, thank you. But, the first half of this slogan is right on the money. There are many priceless moments, priceless experiences, priceless items, and priceless gifts in life. You may have been the giver or the recipient of one or many of these.

There are some priceless things that I've never seen in any of their commercials though. There is one gift in particular that is so priceless, it leaves some people speechless, while other can't keep quiet. Of course, I'm speaking of the most priceless gift of all: salvation.

Jesus is the ultimate gift, and salvation is the absolute highest gift you could ever receive. I'll put it this way. Someone who is given $1,000,000 and has never encountered Jesus has a soul destined to be lost for eternity, whereas a person who hears and responds to the gospel message has a rich destiny indeed. How else will people realize the riches of salvation if someone doesn't give up their time and share this message!

In Acts 3:6, Peter says something shocking to someone who was expecting or at least seeking a monetary gift. There was a man begging for money, and Peter turns to him and says, "Silver and gold have I none; but such as I have give I thee ..." Once this man encounters the power of Jesus Christ, his life is never the same.

But what if Peter didn't stop to interact with this beggar? What if he crossed on the other side of the road? I'm sure being a busy apostle, he had somewhere to be. Well, I'm also sure that Peter knew that there was no better use of his time and God's power than to share Jesus at this moment.

These are the three most eternally impactful ways to give, and they all require your time.

The Gift Which Lasts Forever

Giving your time to lead others to Christ needs to be a regular part of your generosity plan. Mark 2:1-12 describes a day when Jesus was in town and had a crowd gathered at a house. There were so many people that there was no way you could get to Him. That is, unless you were thinking outside of the box—as the people in the story did.

There was a man there who needed a touch from Jesus. This man needed healing, for he could not walk, and like all of humanity, he needed saving from his sins. Jesus, of course, has power to give both. The only way he could get to Jesus was if he had someone else help him to reach Jesus and give up their time and energy for him

He had friends who loved him enough to do whatever it took to get him to the Master. This true story shows how the love and persistence of friends can save one's life for eternity. They carry him to the rooftop of the house, undo the tiles, and lower him right in front of Christ. He gets healed, and more importantly, his sins are forgiven. Now he can count on one day calling heaven his home.

The story goes on but never mentions these friends again. Who are these men who took the time and effort to bring their friend to Jesus? It is incredible to think about the impact they had on one man's life by being completely selfless and not only giving up time but also the strength and muscle necessary. It took faith. It took guts. It took inventiveness. It took patience.

How many men and women, boys and girls, are waiting, searching, yearning, and desperately needing to know Jesus intimately? If only a friend would enter their equation and share some of their time, not wanting or expecting anything in return!

I know I have been caught up too many times with the business of life, passing on an opportunity to lift someone up and bring them to Jesus. How many times have you been the same?

A buddy of mine went beyond spending time. He spent money to be a part of his cousin's encounter with Jesus. He invited her to a Christian concert, bought the tickets, provided transportation, and bought dinner. Some would call this bribery: I call it strategy. That concert opened the door for him to share the gospel and resulted in her accepting the Lord.

Get creative in spending time and resources to share the message of Jesus Christ. Make it fun. But whatever you do, don't pass up on the opportunity.

I always think about how many people I didn't offer this gift to who later died not knowing the Lord. All because I was afraid of what others would think, or because I figured they didn't want to be bothered, or because they didn't accept the gift at a previous time. But now they have no chance to receive.

In 2021, I had the privilege of hearing John Maxwell speak at a one-day event. The event, Work as Worship, is unique because it is centered on the pivotal intersection of working—what we were made to do— and worshiping the One who made us. During John's first hour, he told this story about a time when he began as a pastor in his first church:

> *When I started off as a pastor, evangelism was not my #1 priority. I wanted to help people, of course. I wanted to help people find God, but it wasn't my #1 priority. It was probably in my top ten list but just not number one.*
>
> *That was until a couple of ladies in my congregation who had a very sick brother in the hospital asked me to visit him. Of course I would visit him; that's what pastors do; they visit people in the hospital.*
>
> *I went to visit Jim, and I liked him a lot. He was a nice guy, but he'd never been to church. So, I*

would go and visit him every few days. He was in the hospital for a couple weeks, and we were connecting well. In fact he said, "I really like you, John, we really connect, and when I get out of the hospital, I'm going to come to your church." I told Jim's sisters, and they cried, "Oh, that's so exciting. All we ever wanted is for our brother to come to church!"

One day, I had a really nice conversation with Jim, and then I left and made some other calls, like pastors do. I mean this is a little country church in Southern Indiana, a very small church ... my first church. I got home, and my wife was on the phone, and she said, "Just a moment," to the one she was speaking to. She told me that she was speaking to one of the sisters, and um ... Jim died. I said, "You must be kidding! I was just with him a few hours ago!"

The sisters wanted to know if I would do the funeral, and I said of course I would. I mean that's what pastors do; we do funerals, I've got this funeral stuff down, yeah, I will do the funeral. So a couple days later, they had a viewing. See back then, they would view the body first, so I went with the two sisters to the funeral home to view the remains of their brother. So I'm doing the pastoral thing, just putting my arms around them, just loving them.

And when I look in the casket, at Jim, all of a sudden it hit me ... he's lost. He didn't know God. And John, you were his last chance to know God. You didn't talk about God, you talked about church. As a matter of fact, all you did was talk about church ... come to church, come to church, come to church. Then, I began to weep. I was in an emotional state of awareness that my #1 priority was not sharing my faith with people.

The odds tell me that it's not #1 in your life either. If it was, our behavior would be totally different. Church would not be church as we see it today. Trust me.[2]

John was speaking to an audience of business leaders, and this may have been the most powerful talk on evangelism I've ever heard. In summary, here are the fundamental truths John shared during the first part of this session:

- Sharing your faith should be your #1 priority because it is God's #1 priority.
- If you value people, you will share Jesus with them, and after you add value to them in this way, your relationships will blossom.
- The only people who had a problem with Jesus valuing everyone were the religious people. You see, religious

If you love people and

therefore value them,

you will give them the

greatest gift.

people don't value everyone; they only value their own kind.

- If you value everyone, you need an intentional strategy in sharing your faith. In 1 Corinthians 9, Paul says that he is reaching a wide range of people. So, if you don't have a strategy for sharing your faith outside of church, it is a flawed strategy.

Remember, as I wrote in *Biblical Faith Meets Financial Strategy*, this is about relationship, not religion. If you love people and therefore value them, you will give them the greatest gift. "For God so loved the world, that he gave …," so we could give just like Him. God gives you resources of all kinds, money, talent, time … so you can share Him. Nothing else really matters. Everything else only matters if its purpose is to lead to this regifting moment.

There is one important caveat you probably already realize by now. If you read the section on regifting in the previous chapter, you will see that there is a prerequisite to this type of gift. In order to give something you already have in your possession to someone else, you have to have it yourself. To be effective in regifting Jesus, you must have Jesus. And in this case, since you can give Jesus to everyone you meet and never run out, you get to keep the gift even though you continually share Him.

For those who lead others to Christ, there is a glorious reward in heaven; but don't overlook the substantial reward here on earth. "The fruit of the righteous is a tree of life; and he that winneth souls is wise" (Proverbs 11:30).

Yes, wisdom comes by giving the greatest gift. Winning souls, sharing your true faith in Christ, that's the way to wisdom. Jesus gave us salvation to give away via our testimony. And as a righteous person planting these seeds (like Adam in the beginning in the garden), you will reap the fruit—a great reward indeed— a tree of life.

Yes, with Godly Wisdom comes Godly Wealth. This intersection results in wisdom that is nothing like the corresponding worldly counterfeit. And His wealth is real wealth, and no sorrow comes along for the ride.

I must make sure you have this gift. In fact, I want to give this priceless gift to you if you have not already received Christ in your heart. Just go to salvation.zeroinfinancial.com[3] and read all about it, and don't forget to download the gift I want to give you to help you along the journey.

Now that you have the greatest gift, regift it to someone else. As the title of this book exclaims, we must plan our generosity. So, how are you planning to give your time by sharing Jesus today?

The Gift Which Goes Unnoticed

When you think about the word "worship," what comes to mind? We worship God with praise. We worship God with offerings. We don't normally think of it this way, but we worship God by serving. Worship and serving go hand in hand. Jesus replied to the devil's temptation by exclaiming, "The Scriptures say, 'You must worship the Lord your God and serve only him'" (Luke 4:8 NLT).

Matthew 20:28 says that Jesus did not come to be served but to serve. Jesus' first priority was to serve the Father. This included serving others because it is the Father's will that we serve each other. Serving others is serving God. And serving God is indeed worshiping Him. Just as worshiping our Lord brings peace and joy to our lives, so also does serving others bring genuine joy. Yes, when you give by serving others, you get rewarded with something money can't buy.

Even the world has come to this conclusion: "When we help others we feel happy. There appears to be a direct correlation with overall well-being and giving our time, money or other resources to a cause that we are passionate about. Studies suggest that people who volunteer report better health and more happiness than people who do not volunteer."[4]

Give your time to serve because Jesus came to serve. Christ is the Head of the Church; we are the body. Be the hands and feet of Christ. Have the mind and heart of

Jesus. Remember the principles from *Biblical Faith Meets Financial Strategy - Finances by the Fruit of the Spirit*. You can download a PDF version of this guide from the resource webpage.[5] This guide will remind you how the Holy Spirit will lead you in your financial management. You can see generosity woven into each of the nine Fruit of the Spirit, especially love, kindness, goodness, and meekness.

Serve others right where they are. Serve in your local church. Serve in your community. Serve on the streets of your city. We all need to serve each other in every situation; from life's minor bumps in the road to unfortunate traumatic events. What better way to display love for your fellow humankind and to worship God all at the same time!

Vintage Church in Louisiana shared a blog post on this topic:

> *Why is the act of serving often regarded as work instead of worship? One reason may be that we can become so "works" driven. In our culture today, we constantly stay busy and struggle to rest in God. Jesus calls us to serve not for the sake of being tired and weary, but rather to worship and experience joy. Just as he took joy in washing his disciples feet and demonstrating his love for them, we must do so as well. When we lose sight of the purpose of our service, we can go to God, and allow him to refresh and renew us. John 13 is a powerful passage for us to reflect on in our service.*

*May we serve one another as a demonstration of
an act of worship to God!* [6]

One day, you will pass from this life and find yourself
before the judgment seat of God to give an account. Of
course, there is nothing you could have done and no price
you could have paid to be allowed into heaven. The Great
Judge will not ask you how much you gave to charity, if you
were honest in preparing your taxes, or faithful in
attending Bible study. Only accepting Jesus' sacrifice will
be adequate. And if the Holy Spirit lives in you and
through you, did you display God's love?

Jesus speaking about that day said it this way:

> *Then the King will say to those on his right,
> "Come, you who are blessed by my Father, inherit
> the kingdom prepared for you from the foundation
> of the world. For I was hungry and you gave me
> food, I was thirsty and you gave me drink, I was a
> stranger and you welcomed me, I was naked and
> you clothed me, I was sick and you visited me, I
> was in prison and you came to me." Then the
> righteous will answer him, saying, "Lord, when
> did we see you hungry and feed you, or thirsty and
> give you drink? And when did we see you a
> stranger and welcome you, or naked and clothe
> you? And when did we see you sick or in prison
> and visit you?" And the King will answer them,*

"Truly, I say to you, as you did it to one of the least of these my brothers, you did it to me" (Matthew 25:34-40 ESV).

In order to inherit the kingdom, you must serve as Jesus demonstrated. When you serve, it many times goes unnoticed by people, and rightfully so. But it does not go unnoticed by the Father. Those who do it to be noticed will get no credit because it was done selfishly. The selfless servant, the humble steward, the least here on earth, will be great in heaven.

There was someone at church when the pews were empty, the choir had gone home, and the goodbyes had been said. They were diligently sanitizing the toilets, wiping down the altar, and cleaning the windows. Their work is not work at all: it is service. They didn't do it for the glory and praise from sisters and brothers. Not for money and not for reward here on earth: they are doing it unto God.

The same goes for all those who serve as greeters, musicians, parking ministers, first responders ... the list goes on and on. Many of them fade into the grand orchestration that goes into a Sunday service. Some do things behind the scenes or after hours. There is no clock to punch or paycheck to desire because it is all done for the Glory of God. You were chosen. God has picked you to be on that team and given the gift of service. There are many who are serving right alongside you; but don't believe for a minute that you are not special.

Your local soup kitchen and homeless shelter have people working to keep everything running smooth. We many times don't even know their names. They will never be praised in the local paper, and there will be no viral social media posts about them because servitude is just not that interesting to the masses.

But that is perfectly fine, for we should give our time in service to others because that's what God gave to us. Because we were made in His image, our heavenly Father loves to see His children serve one another.

The Gift Which Originates in the Closet

The third greatest gift you could ever give requires much of your time. We already know that because of your relationship with your Father, He longs for you to come to Him with your requests. As any loving parent here on earth can attest to how natural it is to provide for your children's needs. As I wrote in Chapter 4 of *Biblical Faith Meets Financial Strategy*, you should indeed pray about everything. But, second only to giving God thanks, your prayers should be full of others' requests. Give much time in prayer for others.

The intersection of giving your time and praying for others is called intersession. To intercede is to "stand in the gap." What gap? Sometimes there is a space between our needs and God's provision. Not because God is not willing or able, but because there are spiritual battles that we know

We should give our time in service to others because that's what God gave to us.

not of. Evil would like for us to give up and fall short. But God would like us to be faithful brothers and sisters, helping each other, and praying for one another. By interceding, we can close that gap. As one author writes, "Intercessory prayer takes place in this spiritual world where the battles for our own lives, our families, our friends and our nation are won or lost."[7]

Jesus gave His life on the cross because He is the only living sacrifice which can cover our sins, bridging the gap between us and the Father. As Christians, we must daily take up our cross, being like Christ, by pleading on behalf of others.

Your friends, family, neighbors, coworkers, acquaintances, and fellow brothers and sisters may never know you have given up your time to pray for them. This is many times an anonymous gift. I watched my parents get up in the wee hours to pray. You may have heard the many stories of people praying consistently over a period for their city, their nation, their world, resulting in miraculous outcomes.

And this is something anyone can give. Every person from ministers to elderly widowers to elementary age children can give big, by spending their time before the throne of God for a friend. It takes diligence; it takes persistence; it takes intentionality, but it doesn't cost a penny. If you want to give much without spending money, there is no greater gift.

Your church probably has a prayer request system of some kind. Sometimes there is a pen and paper station where requests can be written on a card which is dropped into a box. This anonymous method serves both members and visitors alike. Or there could be a website or mobile app where one can make their request known. This way is useful to gather the needs of people around the globe.

No matter the structure, you can be someone who contends for these petitions by being on the intercessory team. In the church I attended many years ago, they called it the Prayer Band. People on this team give up a portion of their week, for example, thirty minutes a day, and pray for the request they were randomly assigned. I remember thinking as a young Christian, "This is crazy because I may never know if this need has been met," for I was always thinking of myself. But, after putting in my prayer request and seeing it answered, I realized that someone else was probably thinking the same thing but prayed nevertheless. Who was it that had enough faith to pray for me without needing to see the outcome, I will never know.

This is the gift which originates in the prayer closet. Have you ever found a pair of shoes in the back of the closet that have never been worn still brand new in the box? There is someone who could use that gift, but they will never get it until you take the box out of the closet and give the shoes away. The same holds true for intercessory prayer. It starts every morning in the closet as you seek God for the answers to so many dilemmas. Your prayers fly to heaven along with all the others praying for the same issue.

There are many times you intercede for someone you know personally. They didn't ask for this gift, but you know they need it. A relative with a marriage hanging by a thread. That coworker in the hospital with days to live. Your friend drowning in financial obligations. When you pray for these needs, your faith will be strengthened as you see the answers come to fruition. And know that when things don't turn out as you expected, there are many other pieces to that puzzle that you know not of. Intercession is mysterious because we are refreshed no matter what the result. You are never giving up your time for nothing.

"I exhort therefore, that, first of all, **supplications, prayers, intercessions, and giving of thanks, be made for all men**; for kings, and for all that are in authority; that we may lead a quiet and peaceable life in all godliness and honesty. For this is good and acceptable in the sight of God our Saviour; who will have all men to be saved, and to come unto the knowledge of the truth. **For there is one God, and one mediator between God and men, the man Christ Jesus; who gave himself a ransom for all, to be testified in due time**" (1 Timothy 2:1-6).

Part III

Use Godly Wisdom While Giving God's Wealth

CHAPTER EIGHT

Where Giving Fits into the Budget

One of the questions I get often is: "Where do I fit giving into my budget?" I'm going to cover the principles and strategies that work well for most cases, but there may be a few obstacles you will need to overcome for your specific situation. If you can't sort out your personal plan for generosity after reading this chapter, you may need to schedule a call with a financial coach to get a custom tailored plan.

Before I jump into this principle and explore these tactics, I would like to give you some advice. I will present a few different money management terms and concepts here that may be new to you. There will be definitions presented to help you grasp the concepts, but I implore you to do some further study if necessary. Don't just skim over an idea you don't understand. You must take ownership of your financial stewardship.

This chapter will cover how to fit your generosity goals into your budget. But what if you don't budget? That would be a problem. Budgeting is the most essential wealth management tool because it directs the money God has given you to manage towards the places you want it to go. And as I've said before, no matter your age, wage, or stage, you need to budget.

This book is not an instruction manual for budgeting, and this chapter will assume you do. So, if you don't budget, review and digest the principles in this chapter, but remember that you need to go learn how to put together a money plan with your financial coach, or via a course, or a good book on the subject. You can find ways to do all the above on this book's resource page.

So, are you ready to take action and give?

Giving Fund is a Sinking Fund

You must save up money for gift-giving. I want to bring up a financial term that focuses on OPTIMIZING OUTGO: Sinking Fund. This is defined as "a strategic way to save money by setting aside a little bit each month."[1] We will use a sinking fund to pile up cash to pay for gifts as the need arises. Most dictionaries today would say that a sinking fund is used to pay off debt, but in this case, there is no debt involved in a financial sense. On the one hand, we are going to accumulate money to avoid using debt; therefore, no payments will be due. On the other hand, being obedient to the Word of God, we are showing love, a debt which will never be paid off.

This plan is a systematic process of saving. You should pray with your spouse or accountability partner about the amount you feel led to give away for the year. Remember, gifts don't have to cost any money, so this is only the amount you want to have set aside for presents or donations of money or gifts for which you need to purchase.

For example, if I want to give $1,200 worth of gifts this year, that means I need to designate $100 on my monthly budget. There should be a category for this sinking fund on the OUTGO side of your monthly financial plan. I name this sinking fund, "Giving Fund."

It would be best to practice patience because you will have very little in the fund when you begin to apply this principle. After my second month of saving, I only have two hundred dollars in the account. What happens if I have ten birthdays on my list and want to buy them all fifty-dollar gifts? I must tell myself, "No," and devise a better plan.

This process won't last for long; it may take a few months to build up to the amount needed for each gift-giving occasion. If you never seem to get there, it must be because your annual target amount is too low. Maybe I needed to raise my $1,200 amount to $1,500. In that case, I must adjust something on the budget to make room for the increase of $25 per month in the gift fund category. Yes, that is the opportunity cost.

Many people ask me where they should keep this money. And my answer is always, where it stays liquid and accessible, just like the emergency fund. Since my amount is not extremely large, I don't mind keeping it in my fireproof safe at home. It's secure, and it is readily accessible there. Once it reaches a certain level, I may move it to an FDIC Insured Savings or Money Market account.

The amount is relatively small, and it needs to be accessible without penalty. It would not be wise to handle this fund as an investment. Sinking funds allow you to have designated money on hand for a specific purpose, so you have no temptation to borrow for any reason.

Giving should not be in a moment of pressure and should not be done rashly. If you are ready, God will show you where He wants you to be generous at just the right time. And it will be in proportion to what you have. Remember what Paul said about giving in 2 Corinthians 8:12, "... it is accepted according to that a man hath, and not according to that he hath not."

So be ready at all times to give. But be prepared by saving and budgeting accordingly. Prayerfully Planning is always better than worryingly wanting. Personally, I want to give to everyone who asks, but I know that this is not realistic.

The budget allows you to give yourself permission to give within the limits of your available resources. The sinking fund makes it methodical so that opportunities are not last-minute budget adjustments. "But generous people plan to do what is generous, and they stand firm in their generosity" (Isaiah 32:8 NLT).

Giving can be a budget-buster if you don't have a proactive plan. Too many people borrow money because they forgot that someone's birthday is approaching or Christmas snuck up on them. Use sinking funds to keep this at bay, and the more you give without spending money the easier budgeting to give will be.

Giving Occasions Are Not Emergencies

Doesn't it seem like those gift-giving opportunities just sneak up on you? You thought your budget was all set, and then in the middle of the month, you realize your anniversary is in a few days! Okay, hopefully, that is not the case. But I've seen people bust their budget for birthdays, wedding gifts, baby showers, and many other occasions.

Holidays are not emergencies, so don't even think about tapping your rainy-day fund for Valentine's Day this year. Christmas is still on December 25. Your husband's birthday didn't move. And all those friends who are getting married and having babies cannot dictate how you manage God's wealth.

It is always best to have a strategy, and it's called a Gift Giving Planner. This tool is where you budget your gifts. Plot out a plan of attack for the month and year. Sure, you will have times when you need to adjust the planner if things pop up. But impulse events and parties can't take over your bank account any longer.

Begin by writing all the ideas where you can give without spending much. This list includes ways you can share your time, talents, and hospitality. Don't hold back on this master list. You can come back and add to this list throughout the year. But it will be nice when you can't think of a gift idea, to have this list ready. Remember that these are some of the most priceless gifts you can ever give.

Next, create a second master list of things you can find to regift, reuse, and repurpose. This list will undoubtedly grow and shrink as you purge your closets, cabinets, and cupboards of all the things you have forgotten you had. You might even divide this list into the location they are in for easy finding, i.e., bedroom, kitchen, etc.

Now comes the benefit of the planner. You can use a calendar or just a simple piece of paper for this step. Write each of the next twelve months, and divide each month into three sections: (1) Family members, (2) Non-family members (Friends, Co-workers, neighbors, etc.), (3) Church & Charity.

Then, you can list all the birthdays, anniversaries, holidays, events, and other gift-giving occasions in each of these sections. As you find out about new ones, you can change the planner as you go. This tool is a living document and needs to stay fluid.

Last, fill in the blanks alongside your budget. Don't forget to pray over these choices as you make them. Prayer must lead you as you plan.

What are you going to give to each of these people or places as the year progresses? Will you have enough money in the fund to buy something expensive? Maybe you could buy something less costly? Or you might find that you can go to your two lists and pick out something that costs nothing at all!

It's so freeing when you get to March, and there are six gift-giving occasions, but it is all in the plan. You don't have to rush and overspend on something they will forget about a few weeks after you give it to them. The quality of your gifts will go up, and the amount you spend goes down. I've found that I give more than ever, while saving money along the way.

When there is a random opportunity to give that you could not have planned for, you must go back to your giving budget. Just like your main financial plan, you must make adjustments along the way. And this also applies to spontaneous generosity.

For example, your cousin needs help and could really use $500 this week to get through. You have prayed with your wife and your cousin during this dilemma, and God is leading you to give the money in this time of need. This is assuming you have the money available in your giving fund.

Now you must go to your grand plan and adjust your giving. You have $500 less that will be available for future occasions. Maybe you have very little to change, or possibly there are several gifts that will need to be adjusted. It all depends on how far along you are on your journey. I call it prosperity maturity.

You have prayed through this process and know that God had led you to these decisions. It takes practice, and you may not have it down to a science for a few months. So be patient with yourself. Give yourself grace and know that this is how you plan your generosity with God's divine provision.

The bottom line is knowing how much you have for this month's and year's budget. Don't let giving this year upset your long-term plan. "Be thou diligent to know the state of thy flocks, and look well to thy herds" (Proverbs 27:23).

Download the Gift Giving Planner template from the resource page: zeroinfinancial.com/intersection.[2]

Think Long Term When it Comes to Kid's Gifts

With giving to your kids, you must think long term. Sure, they want everything off of every shelf from aisle 2 to aisle 11. But is that best for them? And is it in the budget?

You must think, pray, and plan. As Proverbs says, "The thoughts of the diligent tend only to plenteousness; but of every one that is hasty only to want" (Proverbs 21:5). This is a great time to teach your child how to tame their "want" so later they can enjoy "plenteousness."

And, not only should you think about your own opportunity costs, but this is also a great time of year to teach the kids about opportunity cost.

If your daughter says she wants items A, B, and C for Christmas, this may be a situation where you know it would not be beneficial for her to have all three at one time. Let her know you can't have everything all the time in life. So, if she wants two of these choices, which one does she want to give up?

Your daughter will learn that with every choice she makes, there will be other choices she must forgo. This teaching moment will help develop the habit early and curb our natural ability to be spoiled brats.

When we have to wait, we appreciate things more. So, your daughter will be thrilled when she receives the third item for her birthday, which is two months after Christmas.

Also, with kids, we need to give gifts that have a more lasting impact. Experiences are many times worth more than plastic stuff. We should take advantage of volunteer opportunities at Christmas, or any time of year, teaching our kids the value of giving our time. Writing letters to our kids that they may keep forever is a better gift than video games that will collect dust four months from now.

Greg Vaughn says it best in his book, *Letters From Dad: How to Leave a Legacy of Faith, Hope, and Love for Your Family.* In Chapter 2, he writes:

> *I swore right then and there that I would bless my children. Still, telling them verbally seemed redundant. I've done that their whole lives. No, I wanted to leave something behind. Something permanent. And that brought me to the idea of writing a letter. If one letter was good, then two had to be better. And then three and four and five. That's it! I'd write them letters for the rest of my life! So many letters it would take them the rest of their lives just to read them all! They would be poignant letters, filled with what was important to me and why I loved them, and about my hope and dreams and wishes for them—tons and tons of letters.*[3]

This manuscript is the textbook on how to leave one of the best gifts you could ever give. The different letters the author walks the readers through are priceless and impactful. They are suitable for presents today or for leaving in your legacy box. It exhibits the paradox I described earlier that the most precious and appreciated gifts don't cost a dime but cost much time.

The second to last idea I want to touch on surrounds spending money on gifts. When you think long term, you may begin to see things that can build up over time. For example, get your child interested in a series of books, where they look forward to getting the next installment each year to add to their collection. Or you could stir their imagination for history, or science, or the Bible, by using a theme to bring meaning to each present.

Last, my mother taught me that the best way to give to kids, where I was the test dummy in this scenario, is to provide three types of gifts at one time. One present was something that I needed, like a new coat. The second was something that I wanted, like a new bike. And for the third gift, I received something that would help me grow as I approach adulthood, for example, a non-fiction book about using God's Wealth with God's Wisdom. If only this book existed thirty years ago!

Divide and Conquer

A giving strategy that needs to be put into practice more often is divide and conquer. There are several ways to do this. The benefit is to save money when you can't buy for every occasion.

Dividing and conquering comes from a strategy used by the military in battle. I'm sure you have seen this in history books or even in movies. But of course, the Bible has plenty of examples. One of the first times this tactic was used was when Joshua conquered Ai. (Joshua 8:5-7). Part of the army took care of one front, while the other part took care of the rest. You can employ this same approach in giving.

For instance, for friends, spend money only on a few of them and give gifts that don't cost money for the rest. Then the next year, rotate and spend money on the ones you didn't last year, giving cherished hand-crafted gifts that don't cost a penny to the others. You could even choose to give everyone gifts of time, talent, and hospitality for Christmas but spend a little on each for their birthdays throughout the year. The point is the same: you only have so much room in the budget for gifts.

I always think it is a good idea to have a gift exchange. This strategy works incredibly well in the workplace. You can randomly choose a name revealing the receiver of your gift. Or everyone can bring a wrapped gift to the party, and then you play a game to select a present from the pile. I like the former over the latter because you can buy a gift that is especially fitting for your designated recipient. The exchange game can sometimes lead to some hard feelings though.

The other way to divide and conquer is to partner with other family members. Get mom or granddad a big special gift by teaming up with your other siblings where everyone contributes. I've seen cases where each household gives one present for each of the other homes. In this way, you can concentrate on gifts the whole family can enjoy together. We could all certainly use more together time rather than everyone on their mobile devices in their own room time.

As with all things, communication is key. Let your friends, family, and coworkers know they are loved and that you give according to what you have and nothing more. They should know that you expect nothing in return. It is not a competition, and no one owes anyone anything but love.

"Owe nothing to anyone—except for your obligation to love one another" (Romans 13:8a NLT).

Everyone should only give from their heart. We need to talk about this stuff more. During your next budgeting meeting with your spouse and/or accountability partner, bring up generosity and how it will fit in your long-term plan. If there are some large gifts you plan to give, discuss how dividing and conquering could be the answer.

And, as always, pray. God desires that you be a big giver, but within the boundaries of His provisions. He will provide according to His generosity plan for your life. Give at the speed of cash, and you will never regret it.

CHAPTER NINE

Three Ways to Give

No matter if you are giving to church, charity, someone in desperate need, or a friend or family member on their birthday, there are three ways you can give. After considering all the many resources you can give from, whether it be your time or talent or money or hospitality, now you must pray about how and when to give that gift.

Regular Gifts and Offerings

As I mentioned in Chapter 8, bringing an offering to your local church should be a part of your regular giving. If you have a Giving Fund set up as part of your budget, it can come out of this money just like all other giving.

The regular offering is established from the beginning, as you read in Chapter 3. You give regularly out of obedience to the Holy Spirit. Showing your love for God, people, community, and your home church's mission is essential for a healthy financial plan. Regular offerings are a time of honor and worship.

The book of Leviticus describes several types of offerings. The crucifixion of Jesus Christ, dying on the cross once and for all, entirely fulfills many of these offerings. Jesus is our sin offering, the burnt offering, and the guilt offering.

In the days of the Old Testament, God's people would many times bring grain offerings. As stated on Seedbed.com, "The purpose of the Grain Offering was a voluntary expression of devotion to God, recognizing His goodness and providence."[1] The grain offering was a free-will offering. Levitical law did not require any specific frequency of the grain offering. You get to decide how much and how often you give at church. Offering time is worship time.

I must repeat myself, though: the offering is not the tithe. Return the tithe before you spend, save or give. Then plan your giving in the budget, which includes offerings. I only repeat myself because many miss the distinction here.

You cannot give what is not yours. Leviticus 27:26 reads, "You may not dedicate a firstborn animal to the

Lord, for the firstborn of your cattle, sheep, and goats already belong to him." (NLT). Obey and return the tithe, but then you have the chance to give from the rest.

This act of giving is a love offering. You will read this reference many times in the Bible. And don't worry if you don't see the amount of money you feel led to give out of your budget. Your very life can be an offering to God! "I beseech you therefore, brethren, by the mercies of God, that ye present your bodies a living sacrifice, holy, acceptable unto God, which is your reasonable service" (Romans 12:1).

Here, in Romans, Paul presents the idea of serving as an offering. Yes, you can give your time, talent, and hospitality as an offering in the name of the Lord. Indeed, Jesus loves you so much, He came to serve. You can show your love in the same manner. Check out this true story:

> *It was a few weeks ago in my home church on a typical Sunday … What stood out for me was the family seated next to me, a dad, a mom, a daughter, and a son whom I didn't recognize. Based on the boy's movements and the attentions given him by his mother and sister, the son seemed to have some form of autism, maybe Asperger's syndrome.*
>
> *His foot and leg were bouncing almost constantly, calming only momentarily when his mother gently touched his knee, which she did every five or ten minutes. Before and after communion,*

he crossed himself repeatedly. He sang with more enthusiasm than musical ability, but if one must choose, that's the one to have.

The moment that really touched me came at the offering.

He didn't have money, but when I handed him the basket, he bowed toward it. At first I thought he was reverencing the basket as if it were an icon or some other holy thing. But then he leaned forward even more, placing the basket on his knees and nearly touching his forehead into the checks, bills, and envelopes inside. His family didn't intervene, as if this were his normal routine. Then he sat up again and handed the basket to his mother.

Suddenly, it dawned upon me: he was putting himself in the offering basket, diving in head-first, if you will. And this must be what he does every week, his own self-made ritual.

And at that moment, I was awash in a baptism of grace.[2]

The same passion goes for all the gifts you give to charities and organizations who are changing the world for the better. Charities depend on people who understand that they have been blessed to be a blessing. Though they will surely appreciate a check, serving a nonprofit by volunteering your time may be more valuable than any amount of money you can give.

By the way, for cash gifts to church and charity, it is not somehow more righteous to give without your name on it. Indeed, give by check or write your name on the envelope if it is cash. And keep a detailed account of your generosity. The recipient is not getting more or less because the gift is anonymous.

By reporting it, you are in effect putting Caesar in his proper place. You see, even the government will bow to God on the tax form when you deduct charitable gifts. When you fail to report it, those funds are taxed. But, when you do, you can now give more. Do the math!

Outside of church and charity, we have many other opportunities to give. There is an entire global industry built around regular times of giving. Of course, you can name the holidays with little thought because there are advertisements on billboards, on the Internet, and at every radio and television commercial break. Valentine's Day, Easter, Mother's Day, Father's Day, and Christmas top the list when it comes to dollars spent. But surprisingly—at least to me—I find people caught off guard when that special day approaches.

Holidays are predictable annual events that should be added to your financial plan. These opportunities to spend on others should not be a shock to your budget. So, if you have not planned enough money for the presents you want

Holidays are predictable annual events that should be added to your financial plan.

to present, never fear, you now know from Part II in this book how to give big without spending much.

Don't forget those special days which you have in all caps on your phone's calendar. Baby showers, weddings, anniversaries, birthdays, retirement celebrations, grand openings, graduations, promotions, house warming parties, and on and on. These are all regular giving opportunities, though some are once in a lifetime. They all can be planned for, added to the budget, saved up for, and strategically established in your overall money management scheme.

The beginning of a new year is a great time to sit down and fill out your Gift Giving Planner. That way, there are no surprises. Total it all up and divide it by 12. This is the amount you need to save each month just to cover your family's regular gifts and offerings this year. Is the number larger than expected or greater than the giving line on your budget? Now you know you must make adjustments. Welcome to being a responsible adult and a faithful steward of God's resources.

This conflict in generosity planning is what most people don't face. They go through life, allowing giving moments to spring upon them, knocking them off their plan, or lack thereof. But not you!

You know you can make something special to give to your grandchild for graduation, for which you paid hardly any money, but cost you time, patience, and love. The opportunity cost may dictate that you cut back on your

Vacation Fund to increase your Giving Fund this year. Now you are at peace and have no guilt when you show up at your cousin's wedding with no material gift, no lame excuses, and no apologies. And there will be times you withhold the little money you could give, and instead give a bit of your life.

You are honest with God, yourself, and others. It's all in the plan and where generosity and reality intersect.

Spontaneous Gifts

When you see someone in need and the Holy Spirit speaks, it's your chance to be used by God at that moment. It is a good thing you have been saving up in your giving fund for months or maybe years. You have been waiting for a time such as this.

Have you ever wondered how people can react to a need at a moment's notice? You know, from the beginning of this chapter. It's called praying, saving, and waiting. Being prepared seemed so dull until now.

I've been in that church service before. There is a special guest, a missionary who has been gone for over a year. They have been working in a small village you have never noticed on the globe. The family gives a presentation with pictures and videos from the people they are reaching for Jesus. You see the tremendous impact they are having. And you feel a tug on your heart.

The most significant investment you can make is to help spread the message of Jesus Christ to the unreached. Investing your time and relaying your testimony to others is the best use of your time. Using your God-given talent to create the tools needed for these endeavors is why you were born with them. And, of course, the wealth you are stewarding is best invested in the same.

Giving to the mission field is one way to invest in the kingdom. "For they are traveling for the Lord, and they accept nothing from people who are not believers. So we ourselves should support them so that we can be their partners as they teach the truth" (3 John 1:7-8 NLT).

This moment of spontaneity doesn't just come while at church; it may appear at any moment. There are charities I felt led to give to after a presentation during a music concert. A letter in the mail or an email may arrive with a need that you are in the perfect position to fulfill.

I've also been in the same situation where there was a call for generosity, and I felt regretful for not planning because I could not take part. That's not God. The Holy Spirit is a gentleman, and those moments of disappointment were all self-inflicted. Don't fall for this trap.

Those moments when I could not financially give only drove me to get ready for the next moment. Your heart and your bank account must be ready. I know Matthew 24:42 is referring to Jesus coming back to take us home. But could you apply this in this light of giving? "Watch therefore: for ye know not what hour your Lord doth come."

What if the Lord comes to you with a need? Are you ready to give your service to someone who needs your skills? Will you have the funds available for that neighbor with an expensive medical burden? Is your schedule freed up for the Lord to use to do a miracle? Please don't beat yourself up as I did when I was not ready. Just start preparing for the next need. I promise you there is another one right around the corner.

In *God's Ownership Meets Money Management*, I mention a not-so-good story of a customer committing financial infidelity right before my eyes. Well, at the same gas station that I worked, there was another situation that I got to witness which made my day.

A gentleman was buying a few things, and he tried to pay with a card, but it was declined. As he turned to walk out of the store empty-handed, a young lady was behind him and yelled, "No, I got it!" He looked stunned and whispered, "Are you sure?" He left the store super appreciative.

After he was gone, I thanked the young lady and mentioned how she was such a blessing. I didn't expect a response.

She then told me that one day twelve years ago she was hungry and was trying to buy a sandwich and a beverage at a store, but her card was declined. She was starving and almost in tears. Then a gentleman behind her said, "I got it!" She was so thankful because her need was real. She never forgot all these years later. The effect of generosity was her reason; paying it forward was the result.

Later in the year, my wife and I had an opportunity to spontaneously be a blessing. After moving to a new apartment complex, we knew we would not be traveling to see relatives or having any friends or family come visit for the usual Thanksgiving feast. So, we asked our new neighbors what they were doing, and several of them responded with a surprising answer: "We are going to spend the holiday alone." During this second year of pandemic restrictions, it seemed as if loneliness was the prevailing symptom, making it a challenging time for many people. What a perfect time to be neighborly!

Being crafty, my wife used her talent to make special invitations with some supplies we already had and invited the seven other units in our building over for a Friendsgiving potluck! We wouldn't have to spend any money above and beyond what we would have spent on just the two of us. But we would invest time and love in order to give the gift of hospitality.

At the time we were planning this, I did not know how impactful it would be. One gentleman confessed he had not been able to celebrate the holidays since his mother passed a few years prior. Another neighbor was so moved that she decided to do the same for the upcoming Christmas evening. Giving is contagious!

Manage the wealth

God has entrusted to

your hands well,

prayerfully plan,

and be ready to

generously give at a

moment's notice.

Also, I didn't really think about it until writing this chapter; we were celebrating this special day with neighbors on the 400th anniversary of the very first Thanksgiving, and it was indeed a day of spontaneous generosity.

In a Fox News report, the writer states:

> *The First Thanksgiving is a heroic tale about a moment in time when two disparate peoples found a way to come together in harmony and respect. The Pilgrims' story teaches courage, persistence, love of liberty and gratitude to God. The Wampanoag demonstrated generosity, neighborliness and friendship in their offers of assistance to the newcomers. We and subsequent generations of Americans can continue to learn from the First Thanksgiving and be inspired by it.*[3]

There will be another point when you and I will be confronted with a chance to bless someone soon. We don't know when it will be or how it will be presented to us. All we can do is manage the wealth God has entrusted to our hands well, prayerfully plan, and be ready to generously give at a moment's notice.

Outrageous Gifts

The first way to give was very planned and systematic. The second was spontaneous and random. Both are strategic, though, because God is an orderly God. Your giving needs to be methodical.

Well, that is no truer than in outrageous giving. I have never been used in this way yet, but I can't wait to be. You must be organized and very much prayed up to be available and willing to give enormous sums of time, talent, hospitality, or money.

It is no small task to pay for an entire community center, or open your home to a half dozen refugees at once, or write a seven-figure check. But there are people ready and willing to do the work of God. Some of these events take long periods of planning, and others can happen overnight.

To go deeper into this area of generosity, I wanted to learn from someone who lives this out in his life every day. I had the privilege to interview Jamey Paugh, who has a thriving ministry which "inspires individuals and organizations to live and give generously, leading to debt freedom, wealth generation, and a fulfilled life!"[4]

> **Johnny:** So when it comes to generosity, and you believe God is speaking to you, how do you know if a prompting to give is from God, or just last night's pizza?

> **Jamey:** For me, I know that prompting because it's something I don't want to do. I am 100% positive that it's outside of the

realm of something; I would just say, "Hey, I want to go and do this, you know, go give that person $5,000." Most likely, I'm not just going to randomly want to give someone $5,000.

And so for me, this has got to be a God thing. Because there's no way I'm going to come up with this myself. And the pizza last night is not gonna tell me to do that either.

It's not the devil either. No, definitely not. Anything that results in thanksgiving to the Lord is not going to come from the enemy. And it's not going to come from, you know, some random, self guided thought. It's going to be Holy Spirit led.

Johnny: So what does it sound like when the Holy Spirit speaks to you about giving—like giving big! I'm talking about giving your house or your car—very large gifts. What does it sound like when the Holy Spirit says, "Here's this big number or big thing"?

Jamey: That's a great question. It comes initially in the form of that outrageous thought of, "Hey, we should give $10,000." And then there is a series that I run through of just questioning and doubting ... like, "That? That's nuts. That's crazy. Why would I give $10,000?" Then it's followed by a sense of peace.

Also, I feel most of the times my heart racing, my inside shaking a little bit. And then faith starts to rise up, and I begin to think about all the good that can come from generosity and how much this gift can impact others.

And then for me, because I'm married, I always confirm it with my wife, because two are one. So I don't make the final jump, the final decision without my wife. You know, nine out of ten times, my wife says she was sensing the same thing before I even asked. And ten out of ten times we've agreed together.

Johnny: You know, Jamey, there's giving and there's generosity: people are generous, and they give to a charity or to the poor or a regular type of offering. But how would you define outrageous or extreme giving?

Jamey: Extreme giving to me is doing more than you can and doing more than others expect. Where I get that is in 2 Corinthians 8:3-4. Paul is talking about giving and says, "I can assure you that they gave as much as they could, and even more than they could. Of their own free will they begged us and pleaded for the privilege of having a part in helping God's people in Judea" (GNT).

I mean, these people were so desperate to give that they were willing to go above and beyond, and as a result, they did more than we expected. First, they gave themselves to the Lord; then they gave themselves to serving because that was what God wanted, meaning, they gave of their resources so that the work of the ministry would see lives changed.

I think outrageous generosity is realizing that I'm partnering my natural resources with the supernatural capabilities of God.

So outrageous is, "I've gone beyond what is humanly possible. And now I'm moving into a place of faith where I'm saying, 'Okay, we're going to give like this, even though we don't think we can.'" That's generosity versus just giving.

So giving is: I saw a need, and I gave.

Generosity is planned. Generosity is a lifestyle, like where you set out and go, "I'm going to give X amount at X time," or "I have determined that I want to give over and above this much money and this much time." So for us, like that's where I set generosity goals, it's a lifestyle for us. At the beginning of the year, we pray, and then we together select a number. "Hey, we want to give this much money this year." And then we select particular organizations that we want to give to. And then on top of that, we leave room for this Holy Spirit moment where we heard about this project, or we heard this story.

But we're planning, and we're calculated, and it's always more than we think is possible.

Johnny: So does outrageous generosity ever get uncomfortable for you? If so, how? If not, then why not?

Jamey: It's always uncomfortable because I'm selfish.

Always, you know, do I want to give my friend $20? Or do I want to keep the $20? You know, do I want to give to x, y, & z projects? Or do I want to keep that money and go on vacation, or buy a pair of shoes? I mean, the reality is, as humans, we're self centered. And we always want to feed ourselves: we are consumers.

But the beauty of generosity is it absolutely destroys that consumer mentality. It gets rid of self centeredness. And it helps you realize that life is not about you, but it's about serving others. And it enables you to be more like Jesus. And so, it's always uncomfortable. It's never initially comfortable. But it makes me more like Christ.

Johnny: So, the last question is, what do you tell someone who wants to yield to the

Holy Spirit and give away everything. They want to empty the bank account, but they're apprehensive and they know the Holy Spirit's talking to them; but they're jittery—which is totally natural. But what do you tell them?

Jamey: If you have heard from the Lord, then do it.

When it comes to emptying a bank account completely, we have done that. We've done it multiple times. And it is a scary, scary, scary proposition. But we also know that we heard from the Lord. All of those things that I talked about previous: communicating together, we agree, the sense of awe, that this is so far above and beyond us. I would never consider doing something like this on my own; I'm too selfish.

You know, when you have walked through the process, and you've spent time praying, and your heart's racing, you just say, "I need to do this, in faith." So you take this step and you trust God. I mean, the reality is that's living inside of God's economy.

His economy is sowing and reaping. And so when I plant a seed, I'm going to reap in His time. So when we plant apple seeds, we get apples; and we sow orange seeds and get oranges. When I plant the seeds of finances, I'm going to reap that—but it's all up to God. And so that's God's kingdom, sowing and reaping. That's not the way of the earth. That's the way of the Lord.

And so, I would encourage somebody when they sense that to go all in, make the leap, make the jump.

Johnny: Awesome! Awesome! All right, thank you so much for that wisdom.

That was a lot of wisdom, and I am so grateful to catch up with him amid his busy life of travel and being a husband and dad to two little ones.

Well, you heard it from the preacher. It's time to start praying and asking God how He would like you to begin giving today, tomorrow, and beyond. And, there is no need for you to be scared. The return on investment is beyond measure. Jesus said, "Sell your possessions and give to those in need. This will store up treasure for you in heaven! And the purses of heaven never get old or develop holes.

When you give lavishly,

all the needs you are

concerned about will be

met, and there will be

plenty more in store.

-Jamey Paugh

Your treasure will be safe; no thief can steal it and no moth can destroy it" (Luke 12:33).

I'll end this chapter with a quote from a message Jamey preached at my church:

> *Generosity changes the world. If you are worried about generosity leaving you without, then the god of comfort, and the god of safety, and the god of security is your god. God says He will never leave you nor forsake you. God sees you. When you give lavishly, all the needs you are concerned about will be met, and there will be plenty more in store.*

CHAPTER TEN

Biblical Patterns
of Giving

I want to end this book exploring God's wealth and God's wisdom with five stories where His people showed great acts of generosity.

Of course, God wants us to give the way He designed it to be done,   and He would never give us a task without the instructions to go along with it. His instruction manual, AKA the Bible, gives us the directions to use and the tasks to do when managing His Wealth.

These five stories are from the Word of God. If you would like a model to pattern your giving after, these may be just for you. Don't skip reading these scriptures. Grab your Bible and read them in other translations to do a deeper study. You may relate to them and be able to apply them to your daily life. Or you may not relate to these examples and therefore need to study and apply these patterns to your future plan and budget. Either way, they will surely bless you.

These Biblical characters were able to be a blessing to others because they were intentional with the resources they were tasked to manage. They all reverenced the Owner and knew their place as stewards.

Purpose Driven Giving

Let's begin with the very familiar story, but look at the giving narrative inside the story. The well-known story is that of the birth of Jesus Christ in that Bethlehem manger. God's one and only Son is the greatest gift ever given. We know that and have shared that story with many people in our lives.

But, as you well know from manger displays erected at Christmas time, there were gift-givers on the scene. Who were those other people traveling to see the newborn King? And why did they go out of their way to arrive at a barn? The wise men came bearing valuable presents to worship the King of kings, Jesus.

"Now when Jesus was born in Bethlehem of Judaea in the days of Herod the king, behold, there came wise men from the east to Jerusalem, Saying, Where is he that is born

King of the Jews? for we have seen his star in the east, and are come to worship him … When they saw the star, they rejoiced with exceeding great joy. And when they were come into the house, they saw the young child with Mary his mother, and fell down, and worshipped him: and **when they had opened their treasures, they presented unto him gifts; gold, and frankincense, and myrrh**" (Matthew 2:1-2,10-11).

Why did they choose such gifts? Because they were giving gifts befitting both a king and a deity. There was a purpose for each gift. The Spirit led them in their gift-giving for sure. We can learn a lot from these wise men.

Christ is King of kings and Lord of lords: therefore, there was the gift of gold. We know about Jesus' deity today; but how did the men have this knowledge? God spoke to them. Items made with gold were associated with royalty in that era, so this present was no ordinary gift.

Bringing frankincense was especially unique because it showed their understanding that Jesus is God. Frankincense was not cheap and certainly not for everyday use. It was used specifically for worship and is listed in the book of Exodus as one of the ingredients used at the temple altar.

Myrrh is an odd gift. This spice was used during the preparation of a body for burial. That would have been a prophetic gift signifying that Jesus would ultimately die for us. Myrrh was also used to prepare the priests and

They were able to be a blessing to others because they were intentional with the resources they were tasked to manage.

instruments in the temple before making a sacrifice. And, as we know, Jesus is our High Priest.

The wise men were spoken to, led, and moved by God in their actions. We need to allow God to speak to us, lead us, and move us in our giving. Remember that these wise men didn't have the Promised One dwelling in us like we now do.

Allow the Holy Spirit to move you, giving you insight into people's lives and situations as you meet them day by day. You will be surprised by the people God puts in your path to serve. There are many in need waiting for you to ask, seek, and pray. God will lead you as you make yourself available for generosity via divine provision.

No matter if it is an offering, a charitable contribution, a present for a family member, or a gift exchange at work, God can use that moment to change that person's life. So, think about each gift's purpose as God gives through you.

Prosperity Driven Giving

In Exodus, we find the account of Pastor Moses collecting an offering for the building of the tabernacle. I'm sure you have heard of or been a part of a building project where there was a specific amount of money needed to complete all the approved plans. This collection is a free-will offering above and beyond other regular offerings and missionary pledges made.

Moses finds himself in a situation that many pastors would love. After collecting and counting, the wise men working under Moses came to him and uttered a phrase I have never heard a leader say: "Stop. No more. We have too much." This passage presents a story of ultra-generosity. When you understand that God owns it all and you have the opportunity to use that divine provision to grow the Kingdom for His purpose, hold nothing back.

"And they received of Moses all the offering, which the children of Israel had brought for the work of the service of the sanctuary, to make it withal. And they brought yet unto him free offerings every morning. And all the wise men, that wrought all the work of the sanctuary, came every man from his work which they made; And they spake unto Moses, saying, **The people bring much more than enough for the service of the work, which the Lord commanded to make.** And Moses gave commandment, and they caused it to be proclaimed throughout the camp, saying, Let neither man nor woman make any more work for the offering of the sanctuary. So the people were restrained from bringing. For the stuff they had was sufficient for all the work to make it, and too much" (Exodus 36:3-7).

This situation is something that should happen all the time in every community. The more people use God's Wealth with God's Wisdom, the wealthier they will become. There will be a surplus because you can't out give God. As people give more, they will prosper and will use that prosperity to give even more. With God's guidance, community centers, libraries, schools, hospitals, and churches can be built with no burdens, no debt, and no worries, as the cycle continues.

This is not something that happens by chance—it's all in the Master's plan. Budget for giving and allow God to direct your path. Be prepared to be used by God, and be prepared to have your life used in ways you never thought possible.

Your neighborhoods are better off when the residents submit to God's plan. The people in this scripture were blessed because they were obedient. They had an abundance because they were giving out of love. God would never have provided for them if He didn't believe they would handle it His way.

Of course, this only applies to true followers of Jesus Christ as members of a church following the will of God. As I mentioned earlier, you need to be in a healthy church. Don't let toxic situations take this privilege away from you.

This story is a great example of a faithful congregation who loved their church. If you are not part of a local community of believers like this, there is one waiting for you. When you serve and use the talents God has blessed you with, the time that God has allotted you, and the wealth God has given you to manage, you will be a blessing to many others, and everyone prospers.

Passion Driven Giving

In 2 Samuel, you will find a powerful story about King David's great and passionate sacrifice to the Lord.

"And Araunah said, Wherefore is my lord the king come to his servant? And David said, To buy the threshingfloor of thee, to build an altar unto the Lord, that the plague may be stayed from the people. And Araunah said unto David, Let my lord the king take and offer up what seemeth good unto him: behold, here be oxen for burnt sacrifice, and threshing instruments and other instruments of the oxen for wood. All these things did Araunah, as a king, give unto the king. And Araunah said unto the king, The Lord thy God accept thee. And the king said unto Araunah, Nay; but **I will surely buy it of thee at a price: neither will I offer burnt offerings unto the Lord my God of that which doth cost me nothing**. So David bought the threshingfloor and the oxen for fifty shekels of silver. And David built there an altar unto the Lord , and offered burnt offerings and peace offerings. So the Lord was entreated for the land, and the plague was stayed from Israel" (2 Samuel 24:21-25).

This piece of history takes place after David sinned and disobeyed God for taking a census of His people. To stay the plague that had come upon the people, David needed a burnt offering to atone for this sin. Praise God, we have Jesus to be that covering we all desperately need!

So, David, being a man after God's own heart, wanted to make these required offerings but wanted to give a financial sacrifice as well. He could have accepted the gift from Araunah; instead he said, "No, I will buy it at a price."

The land David purchased is today known as the Temple Mount. This sacrifice was not just to stop the plague. David was making a sacrifice that would last for thousands of years. He was passionate about having a house of the Lord for many generations. He would later pass it down to his son Solomon to build the permanent temple of God.

Knowing how important the temple would be, David wanted to be sure not to make an offering to God that costs him nothing. So, he paid fifty shekels of silver. He later donated much of the wealth he had in his possession towards building the temple. He offered an estimated amount of between a half-million to a billion dollars in today's US dollars.

David knew the importance of giving, and he led the way. His generous gift would be an example that all the people would follow. I want to be a model of generosity like this. How about you?

When you give, let it be full of passion as you think of its ultimate impact. Give with the hope that it changes people's life, blesses them beyond belief, and is something they never forget. Allow your offerings, pledges, and contributions to influence the next generation. Put thought behind each opportunity as David did, and you will be a steward after God's own heart.

Provision Driven Giving

This fourth story I would like to present is one of outrageous generosity. Giving out of your abundance is an amazing act of charity, and that should be our normal habit. Offerings at church, gifts to those you know, and charitable contributions are all part of setting the tempo of using God's Wealth with His Wisdom. He provides for you, so you can provide for others.

And then sometimes you will do things that seem ridiculous to a non-believer. People with an earthly money mindset may even call you crazy. The early church saw the great needs in the world, and they gave big in response.

"And the multitude of them that believed were of one heart and of one soul: neither said any of them that ought of the things which he possessed was his own; but they had all things common. And with great power gave the apostles witness of the resurrection of the Lord Jesus: and great grace was upon them all. **Neither was there any among them that lacked: for as many as were possessors of lands or houses sold them, and brought the prices of the things that were sold, And laid them down at the apostles' feet: and distribution was made unto every man according as he had need.** And Joses, who by the apostles was surnamed Barnabas, (which is, being interpreted, The son of consolation,) a Levite, and of the country of Cyprus, Having land, sold it, and brought the money, and laid it at the apostles' feet" (Acts 4:32-37).

You know I always say to do all things with prayer. That includes giving five dollars to a homeless woman on the corner, and that certainly applies here. Pray and allow God to speak to you about extravagant gifts.

God may allow you to build up wealth as a provision for some need in the future you know not of. But you can only be in this position if you have been a faithful steward, planned well, and stayed in tune with the Provider.

There are too many people starving worldwide, and you can find many of them in your city. How can we allow there to be homeless veterans? Clean water is the most basic necessity, yet there are countries in dire need. What would you do if God prompted you to part with some of your possessions to provide for others in desperate need? Is your heart ready for the moment the Lord of all provision asked you to make a great sacrifice?

Don't be rash. Use wisdom. If God is calling you to fill one of the countless voids, it would be wise for you to pass it by your pastor or a mentor or two for their prayer and guidance. Being married, you must be in one accord with your spouse when it comes to a gargantuan gift (or any gift, for that matter). And then, if it seems good to them, what a great privilege for you to be used by God in this way!

God loves when

we give willingly,

and He loves

when we give our all.

Power Driven Giving

God loves when we give willingly, and He loves when we give our all. But God knows it takes faith to give everything away. You must have a real relationship with God and know that He will provide for all your needs. As Jesus said, you must have the simple faith of a child (Matthew 17:20).

This event is one of my favorite scenes in the Bible. Jesus has just finished healing a multitude of people from all kinds of sickness and disease. He has performed many miracles, and now the people are hungry. So, Jesus didn't dare let this teaching opportunity pass by.

You will see the disciples' faith tested, and their eyes opened once Jesus uses the offering of a young boy to provide for the masses.

"When Jesus then lifted up his eyes, and saw a great company come unto him, he saith unto Philip, Whence shall we buy bread, that these may eat? And this he said to prove him: for he himself knew what he would do. Philip answered him, Two hundred pennyworth of bread is not sufficient for them, that every one of them may take a little. One of his disciples, Andrew, Simon Peter's brother, saith unto him, **There is a lad here, which hath five barley loaves, and two small fishes**: but what are they among so many? And Jesus said, Make the men sit down. Now there was much grass in the place. So the men sat down, in number about five thousand. And Jesus took the loaves; and when he had given thanks, he distributed to the disciples, and the disciples to them that were set down; and likewise of the fishes as much as they would. When they were filled, he said unto his disciples, Gather up the fragments that remain, that nothing be lost. Therefore they gathered them together, and filled twelve baskets with the fragments of the five barley loaves, which remained over and above unto them that had eaten" (John 6:5-13).

We could be like Philip and not see any possibility. Or, we could be like Andrew, who thought to bring up the possibility but had uncertainty. But, this little boy brought all that he had with no hesitation from what we can tell.

That's all God needs us to do. Just bring all you have, no matter how little. Because little in the hands of God is much. Have the faith of a little child.

Remember that the disciples just witnessed Jesus heal the blind, the dumb, the lame, and cast out demons of all kinds. The crowd followed Him "because they saw his miracles which he did on them that were diseased" (John 6:2). But they didn't believe provision was possible in the moment.

I'm not just saying this to be hard on them. This is me. And this is you. We do this all the time. God does unbelievable things in our lives, and then we hit a snag, and our faith dissipates.

So, Jesus teaches a lesson we must never forget. He takes the young boy's lunch, He asks the Father to bless it as He gives thanks, and then ... He gives it to the disciples.

Then, as the disciples pass out the food, that's where the miracle unfolds: it multiplies.

Don't miss this lesson. Jesus blesses the food and then places it in your hands. God blesses your house and then places it in your hands. The Lord blesses your time and talent; then places them in your hands. The Creator of the Universe has blessed you with His Wealth and placed it in your hands.

Your loving Father in Heaven has blessed your life, so you can be a blessing. He wants you to be a part of the miracle. You are His miracle. So now go give yourself away.

Because You Have Given

God is so good and teaches us so much about handling all the resources made available to use. Throughout this book, you have seen the many attributes of God. I am going to conclude by looking at three of His many names.

As Creator, God is the Master Architect and maker of all things, even us! He exists outside of time, space, and matter; because if He didn't, He wouldn't be able to create it. God is all-knowing, omnipresent, and omnipotent. He is El Shaddai, The All-Mighty.

God is the Giver of Life, so we owe all things to Him. If He owns it all, He gets to make the rules and has all authority to tell us the best way to use everything, including money, talent, time, and our lives. He is beyond rich because He owns all the wealth and those who manage the wealth.

Also, as Creator, God gets to judge His Creation. We don't tell God what He can or cannot do. God is the boss. But since He is perfect in all His ways, He is a gracious and merciful Master. He loves us and would never control us like a tyrant. Therefore, we have our own will to obey and follow or turn our backs and (try) to manage on our own.

As Savior, we see God come to the rescue because we simply made a mess. Like any loving Father, He provided a solution to the problem, a permanent solution in sending the perfect sacrifice of Jesus Christ, His only begotten Son.

Jesus is also called Emmanuel, which means "God with us," because He knew we would need a Teacher, a Mentor, and a Guide. God the Creator gave us life, and God With Us gives us abundant life and the promise of eternal life.

The Father demonstrated the greatest gift ever given by being separated from His one and only Son for a time. It was all to redeem us, be with us, and commune with us. That's true love.

Now He compels us to do the same for others. Look for opportunities. Love your neighbor.

Last, as a Provider and Giver of All Things, the Great Teacher shows the right way to give continually. We call Him Jehovah Jireh because He is faithful to feed us when we are hungry, clothe us when we are naked, provide us with hospitality when we are homeless, and more, if only we would believe.

The provision is free of payment and available to all people. But, there are so many who need to hear this message, so they need suffer no longer. He has tasked us to take care of all His resources; but maybe the most precious of them all is His message. It's up to you and me to carry this hope into all the world. There are people desperate for it and waiting.

In Chapter 7, I presented the scene in which Jesus receives you before the throne of the Highest and says:

> *Come, you who are blessed by my Father, inherit the kingdom prepared for you from the foundation of the world. For I was hungry and you gave me food, I was thirsty and you gave me drink, I was a stranger and you welcomed me, I was naked and you clothed me, I was sick and you visited me, I was in prison and you came to me (Matthew 25:34-36 ESV).*

That is what it looks like when you are living according to the riches of the Word of God. It is a beautiful thing when we do it God's way. So, go manage the resources you will be accountable for at the INTERSECTION of God's Wealth and God's Wisdom.

Free Resources

To help you Zero In on the INTERSECTION where God's Wealth meets God's Wisdom, download the free resources from the INTERSECTION Resource Page:

intersection.zeroinfinancial.com

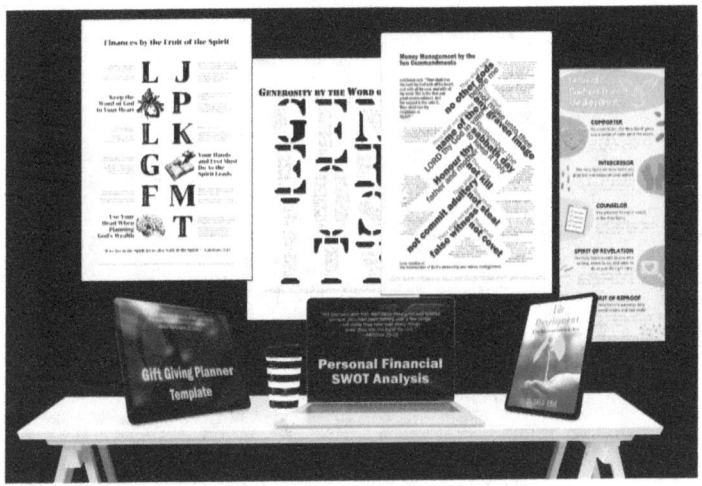

- **BOOK:** Life Development—A New Believer's Guide to Growing in Christ

- **INFOGRAPHIC:** Financial Guidance from the Holy Spirit

- **POSTER:** Finances by the Fruit of the Spirit

- **WORKBOOK:** Personal Financial SWOT Analysis

- **POSTER:** Money Management by the Ten Commandments

- **WORKBOOK:** Gift Giving Planner Template

- **POSTER:** Generosity by the Word of God

Thank You!

To all those who have been so generous to financially support the creation of this book series, I am so thankful. You helped bring INTERSECTION to fruition.

Forward Church Myrtle Beach

Kuba Wyrobek

Clovers & Val McWilliams

Carlos & Maria Correa

Ellie Markova

Anton & Aleksandra Zhloba

Pastor Chris, Heather, & Nelson Honeycutt

Dr. Anthony Jenkins

Pastor Allen & Debbie Causey

D.S. & Stella Wilson

D. Greg & Susie Ebie

David & Kelly Franco

Nicholas Ryan Rendleman

Kaffa Morales

Scott Petrarca

Marcos & Mireya Bernal

Angel Christopher

Pastor Steve & Jessica Mueller

Nick Kolovos

Anibal & Joelia Maldonado

David Gumins

J. Varghese

Linda Ostrowski

Steve & Traci Hickman

Richard L. Dobbins, Jr.

Pastor Edgar & Christie Rivas

Christian Baird

John Kuntharayil

Vuong Dinh

Chaplain James F. Burling

Adele van der Lecq

Edgar Rios

Note from the Author: Reviews are gold to authors! If you have enjoyed this book, would you consider reviewing it on your favorite book retailer's website? Thank you!

Notes

Chapter One: God is a Giver

[1] Laue, Richard. "The Attraction of the Exceedingly Great and Precious Promises of the Bible." Sermon Search. Accessed January 18, 2022. https://www.sermonsearch.com/sermon-outlines/18642/the-attraction-of-the-exceedingly-great-and-precious-promises-of-the-bible/

[2] Alcorn, Randy. "When We See Jesus Face to Face: What Will It Be Like?" Preach It, Teach It (blog). Accessed January 18, 2022. https://preachitteachit.org/articles/detail/when-we-see-jesus-face-to-face-what-will-it-be-like/

[3] "Sinner's Prayer." In Wikipedia, December 27, 2021. https://en.wikipedia.org/wiki/Sinner%27s_prayer#Billy_Graham

[4] McWilliams, Johnny. "Dedicating Your Life to Jesus." Zero In Financial. Accessed January 15, 2022. https://zeroinfinancial.com/salvation/

Chapter Two: The Gift Received When Giving

[1] Malanowski, Jamie. "The Power of Generosity." SUCCESS, November 26, 2015. https://www.success.com/the-power-of-generosity/

[2] Dictionary, Merriam-Webster. "Warm Fuzzies | Definition." Merriam-Webster.com. Accessed November 30, 2021. https://www.merriam-webster.com/dictionary/warm%20fuzzies

[3] O'Brien, Ed. "The Joy of Giving Lasts Longer Than the Joy of Getting." Association for Psychological Science, December 20, 2018. https://www.psychologicalscience.org/news/releases/the-joy-of-giving.html

[4] The Bible Says. "Matthew 6:19-21," September 22, 2020. https://thebiblesays.com/commentary/matt/matt-6/matthew-619-21/

[5] Cole, Pastor Steven J. "Giving God's Way." Bible.org, September 4, 2013. https://bible.org/seriespage/lesson-5-giving-god-s-way-selected-scriptures

Chapter Three: Why Offerings?

[1] Oxford Advanced American Dictionary. "Grudgingly | Definition." Accessed January 18, 2022. https://www.oxfordlearnersdictionaries.com/us/definition/english/grudgingly?q=grudgingly

[2] Brown, Gregory. "The Right Perspective on Supporting Missions." Bible.org, October 7, 2016. https://bible.org/seriespage/17-right-perspective-supporting-missions

[3] Roberts, Mark. "Worship & Money." Church Leaders (blog), December 11, 2011. https://churchleaders.com/worship/worship-articles/156649-worship-money.html

Chapter Four: No Shame in Not Giving

[1] McWilliams, Johnny. "Zero In On This | Demolish Debt." Zero In Financial. Accessed March 13, 2020. https://zeroinfinancial.com/demolishdebt

[2] Wong, Brittany. "This Is When Gift-Giving Becomes Toxic For Families." HuffPost Life, December 12, 2019. https://www.huffpost.com/entry/gift-giving-competition_l_5df2769be4b024ea5ac6f381

Chapter Five: Give Without Spending a Penny

[1] Betty. "Talents and Gifts - 5 Reasons Why You Should Use Them for God." All Round Jesus (blog), March 11, 2019. https://allroundjesus.com/talents-and-gifts-5-reasons-why-you-should-use-them-for-god/

[2] Tobin, Phil. "Volunteering (Giving Time and Talent) Is a Transformational Experience." IGiftFund (blog), April 9, 2020. https://igiftfund.org/blog/volunteering-giving-time-talent-transformational-experience/

Chapter Six: Give Without Spending A Lot

[1] McWilliams, Johnny. "Zero In Financial Press | INTERSECTION." Zero In Financial. Accessed April 4, 2020. https://zeroinfinancial.com/press/intersection

[2] TotebagFactory. "How to Reuse Gift Bags - 19 Ideas and Tips." Accessed January 18, 2022. https://totebagfactory.com/blogs/news/how-to-reuse-gift-bags-ideas

[3] McConnell, Shayla. "60 Ways to Repurpose & Reuse Old Picture Frames." The Home Route, January 11, 2019. https://www.thehomeroute.com/28-ways-to-reuse-recycle-old-picture-frames/

[4] DIY Projects by Big DIY Ideas. "41 Repurposed Items Looking Better Than the Original," May 31, 2017. https://bigdiyideas.com/41-repurposed-items-looking-better-original/

Chapter Seven: The Greatest Gifts You Could Ever Give

[1] Vizard, Sarah. "How Mastercard's 'Priceless' Campaign Became Part of the Brand DNA." Marketing Week (blog), September 19, 2019. https://www.marketingweek.com/mastercard-priceless-campaign/

[2] Maxwell, John. "Change Your World Part 1." Presented at the Work As Worship Retreat, Rockwall, Texas, May 14, 2021.

[3] McWilliams, Johnny. "Dedicating Your Life to Jesus." Zero In Financial. Accessed January 15, 2022. https://zeroinfinancial.com/salvation/

[4] Cassada Lohmann, Dr. Raychelle. "Achieving Happiness by Helping Others." Psychology Today, January 29, 2017. https://www.psychologytoday.com/us/blog/teen-angst/201701/achieving-happiness-helping-others

[5] McWilliams, Johnny. "Zero In Financial Press | INTERSECTION." Zero In Financial. Accessed April 4, 2020. https://zeroinfinancial.com/press/intersection

[6] Weaver, Matthew. "Serving as Worship." Vintage Church of New Orleans, April 12, 2017. http://www.vintagechurchnola.com/blog/2017/4/12/serving-as-worship

[7] The Christian Broadcasting Network. "What Is Intercessory Prayer?," January 23, 2015. https://www1.cbn.com/questions/what-is-intercessory-prayer

Chapter Eight: Where Giving Fits into the Budget

[1] Cruze, Rachel. "What Is a Sinking Fund and How Do You Create One?" Ramsey Solutions, December 17, 2021. https://www.ramseysolutions.com/saving/stop-the-panic-sinking-fund

[2] McWilliams, Johnny. "Zero In Financial Press | INTERSECTION." Zero In Financial. Accessed April 4, 2020. https://zeroinfinancial.com/press/intersection

[3] Vaughn, Greg, and Fred Holmes. Letters from Dad. Nashville Tennessee: Thomas Nelson Publishers, 2005

Chapter Nine: Three Ways to Give

[1] Garrett, Jeremiah K. "The 5 Offerings in the Old Testament." Seedbed (blog), July 29, 2014. https://seedbed.com/5-offerings-old-testament/

[2] McLaren, Brian. "The Church and the Solution." Patheos, November 11, 2011. https://www.patheos.com/resources/additional-resources/2011/11/church-and-the-solution-brian-mclaren-11-11-2011

[3] Kirkpatrick, Melanie. "The First Thanksgiving Story Shows Us How Disparate People Come Together In Challenging Times." Fox News. Fox News, November 8, 2021. https://www.foxnews.com/opinion/first-thanksgiving-story-people-challenging-times

[4] Paugh, Jamey. "GENEROSITY - The Cure For Poverty." Paugh International, January 20, 2022. https://www.jameypaugh.com/

About the Author

Johnny McWilliams, founder of Zero In Financial LLC, guides his students, customers, and clients as they RECOVER from past money mistakes, GROW your present pocketbook position, and ZERO IN on your future financial fortune, ultimately leaving a lasting legacy of love. After working as a tax preparer, dissecting the details of credit scoring and reporting, passing various exams and licensure, including Series 7, Series 66, life & health insurance, and real estate broker, Johnny realized the average American's need for financial coaching, education, and inspiration.

Once Johnny completed ten years of enlistment in the United States Navy, graduated with a Master of Business Administration, worked as a property & casualty insurance consultant, and became certified as a Ramsey Solutions Master Financial Coach, he began guiding individuals and families to Zero In on their financial target.

Johnny and his wife, Christine, have been married for over twelve years, and they are blessed with one married son, one married daughter, and no grandchildren yet.